PENGUIN BOOKS — GREAT FOOD

Eating with the Pilgrims and Other Pieces

CALVIN TRILLIN (1935–) is an American journalist, humorist and novelist. Born in Missouri, he joined the *New Yorker* in 1963. His reporting there has concentrated on America, between the coasts. For fifteen years, he produced an article from somewhere in the country every three weeks, on subjects that ranged from the murder of a farmer's wife in Iowa to the author's efforts to write the definitive history of a Louisiana restaurant called Didee's 'or to eat an awful lot of baked duck and dirty rice trying'.

Eating with the Pilgrims and Other Pieces

CALVIN TRILLIN

PENGUIN BOOKS

PENGUIN BOOKS

Published by the Penguin Group
Penguin Books Ltd, 80 Strand, London WC2R 0RL, England
Penguin Group (USA) Inc., 375 Hudson Street, New York, New York 10014, USA
Penguin Group (Canada), 90 Eglinton Avenue East, Suite 700, Toronto, Ontario,
Canada M4P 2Y3 (a division of Pearson Penguin Canada Inc.)
Penguin Ireland, 25 St Stephen's Green, Dublin 2, Ireland
(a division of Penguin Books Ltd)
Penguin Group (Australia), 250 Camberwell Road,
Camberwell, Victoria 3124, Australia
(a division of Pearson Australia Group Pty Ltd)
Penguin Books India Pvt Ltd, 11 Community Centre,
Panchsheel Park, New Delhi – 110 017, India
Penguin Group (NZ), 67 Apollo Drive, Rosedale, Auckland 0632, New Zealand
(a division of Pearson New Zealand Ltd)
Penguin Books (South Africa) (Pty) Ltd, 24 Sturdee Avenue,
Rosebank, Johannesburg 2196, South Africa

Penguin Books Ltd, Registered Offices: 80 Strand, London WC2R 0RL, England

www.penguin.com

This collection published in Penguin Books 2011

1

Copyright © Calvin Trillin, 1977, 1980, 1981, 1990, 1996,
2000, 2002, 2003, 2010
All rights reserved

Set in 10.75/13 pt Berkeley Oldstyle Book
Typeset by by Jouve (UK), Milton Keynes
Printed in Great Britain by Clays Ltd, St Ives plc

Cover design based on traditional Japanese crackle-glaze plates.
(Photograph copyright © Alamy.) Picture research by Samantha Johnson.
Lettering by Stephen Raw

Except in the United States of America, this book is sold subject
to the condition that it shall not, by way of trade or otherwise, be lent,
re-sold, hired out, or otherwise circulated without the publisher's prior
consent in any form of binding or cover other than that in which it is
published and without a similar condition including this condition
being imposed on the subsequent purchaser

ISBN: 978-0-241-95193-4

www.greenpenguin.co.uk

MIX
Paper from
responsible sources
FSC® C018179
www.fsc.org

Penguin Books is committed to a sustainable
future for our business, our readers and our
planet. This book is made from paper certified
by the Forest Stewardship Council.

Contents

Sources

An Attempt to Compile a Short History of the Buffalo Chicken Wing

I did not truly appreciate the difficulties historians must face regularly in the course of their research until I began trying to compile a short history of the Buffalo chicken wing. Since Buffalo chicken wings were invented in the recent past, I had figured that I would have an easy task compared to, say, medievalists whose specialty requires them to poke around in thirteenth-century Spain and is not even edible. My wife, Alice, I must say, was unenthusiastic about the project from the start. It may be that she thought my interest in pure research could lead me into searching out the origins of just about any local specialty I might contemplate eating too much of – how the cheesesteak got to Philadelphia, for instance, or why Tucson is the center of interest in a Mexican dish called chimichanga, or how people in Saginaw came to begin eating chopped-peanuts-and-mayonnaise sandwiches, or why a restaurant I once visited in the market area of Pittsburgh serves sandwiches and french fries with the french fries inside the sandwiches. I assured her that I had no intention of extending my inquiries as far as chopped peanuts or interior french fries, although I couldn't fail to point out that she had, in a manner of speaking, expressed some curiosity about the Pittsburgh sandwich herself ('Why in the world would anybody *do* such a thing?').

I saw the history of the Buffalo chicken wing as a straightforward exercise, unencumbered by the scrambled folk myth that by now must be part of the trimmings of something like the Philadelphia cheesesteak. There happens to be extant documentation identifying the inventor of Buffalo chicken wings as the late Frank Bellissimo, who was the founder of the Anchor Bar, on Main Street – the form of the documentation being an official proclamation from the City of Buffalo declaring July 29, 1977, Chicken Wing Day. ('WHEREAS, the success of Mr. Bellissimo's tasty experiment in 1964 has grown to the point where thousands of pounds of chicken wings are consumed by Buffalonians in restaurants and taverns throughout our city each week . . .') I would not even have to rummage through some dusty archive for the document; the Anchor Bar has a copy of it laminated on the back of the dinner menu.

I had the further advantage of having access to what people in the history game call 'contemporary observers' – a crowd of serious chicken-wing eaters right on the scene. A college friend of mine, Leonard Katz, happens to be a Buffalonian – a native Buffalonian, in fact, who became a dean at the medical school of the State University of New York at Buffalo. I have also known his wife, Judy, since long before the invention of the chicken wing. She is not a native Buffalonian, but she carries the special credentials that go with having been raised in New Haven, a city that claims to have been the scene of the invention of two other American specialties – the hamburger and the American pizza. Although Leonard Katz normally limits his chicken-wing consumption to downing a few as hors d'oeuvres – a policy, he assured me, that has no connection at all with the fact that his medical specialty is the gastrointestinal tract – the rest of the family think nothing of making an entire meal out of them. Not long before I arrived in Buffalo for my field work, Linda Katz had returned from her freshman year at Washington University, in St. Louis – a city where, for reasons I do not intend to pursue, the local specialty is toasted ravioli – and headed straight for her favorite chicken-wing outlet to repair a four-month deprivation. A friend of Linda's who returned from the University of Michigan at about the same time had eaten chicken wings for dinner four nights in a row before she felt fit to carry on. Judy Katz told me that she herself eats chicken wings not only for dinner but, every now and then, for breakfast – a pattern of behavior that I think qualifies her as being somewhere between a contemporary observer and a fanatic.

On my first evening in Buffalo, the Katz family and some other contemporary observers of their acquaintance took me on a tour of what they considered a few appropriate chicken-wing sources – out of what is said to be several hundred places in the area where Buffalonians can order what they usually refer to simply as 'wings' – so that I could make some preliminary research notes for later analysis. The tour naturally included the Anchor Bar, where celebrated visitors to Buffalo – say, a daughter of the Vice-President – are now taken as a matter of course, the way they are driven out to see Niagara Falls. It also included a noted chicken-wing center called Duffs and a couple of places that serve beef-on-weck – a beef sandwich on a salty roll – which happens to be the local specialty that was replaced in the hearts of true Buffalonians by chicken wings. In Buffalo, chicken wings are always offered 'mild' or 'medium' or 'hot', depending on how much of a dose of hot sauce they have been subjected to during preparation, and they are always accompanied by celery and blue-cheese dressing. I sampled mild. I sampled medium. I sampled hot. It turned out that there is no sort of chicken wing I don't like. As is traditional, I washed down the wings with a number of bottles of Genesee or Molson – particularly when I was sampling the hot. I ate celery between chicken wings. I dipped the celery into the blue-cheese dressing. I dipped chicken wings into the blue-cheese dressing. (I learned later that nobody in Buffalo has figured out for sure what to do with the blue-cheese dressing.) I tried a beef-on-weck, just for old times sake. I found that I needed another order of hot, plus another bottle of Molson. After four hours, the tour finally ended with Judy Katz apologizing for the fact that we were too late for her favorite chicken-wing place, a pizza parlor called Santora's, which closes at 1:00 A.M.

The next morning, I got out my preliminary research notes for analysis. They amounted to three sentences I was unable to make out, plus what appeared to be a chicken-wing stain. I showed the stain to Judy Katz. 'Medium?' I asked.

'Medium or hot,' she said.

* * *

Fortunately, the actual moment that Buffalo chicken wings were invented has been described many times by

Frank Bellissimo and his son, Dom, with the sort of rich detail that any historian would value; unfortunately, they used different details. According to the account Frank Bellissimo often gave over the years, the invention of the Buffalo chicken wing came about because of a mistake – the delivery of some chicken wings instead of the backs and necks that were ordinarily used in making spaghetti sauce. Frank Bellissimo thought it was a shame to use the wings for sauce. 'They were looking at you, like saying, "I don't belong in the sauce,"' he often recalled. He implored his wife, who was doing the cooking, to figure out some more dignified end for the wings. Teressa Bellissimo, presumably moved by her husband's plea, decided to make the wings into some hors d'oeuvres for the bar – and the Buffalo chicken wing was born.

Dom Bellissimo is a short, effusive man who now acts as the bustling host of the Anchor Bar; his friends sometimes call him Rooster. He told me a story that did not include a mistaken delivery or, for that matter, Frank Bellissimo. According to Dom, it was late on a Friday night in 1964, a time when Roman Catholics still confined themselves to fish and vegetables on Friday. He was tending the bar. Some regulars had been spending a lot of money, and Dom asked his mother to make something special to pass around gratis at the stroke of midnight. Teressa Bellissimo picked up some chicken wings – parts of a chicken that most people do not consider even good enough to give away to barflies – and the Buffalo chicken wing was born.

According to both accounts, Teressa Bellissimo cut off and discarded the small appendage on a chicken wing that looks as if it might have been a mistake in the first place, chopped the remainder of each wing in half, and served two straight sections that the regulars at the bar could eat with their fingers. (The two straight pieces, one of which looks like a miniature drumstick and is known locally as a drumette, became one of the major characteristics of the dish; in Buffalo, a plate of wings does not look like a plate of wings but like an order of fried chicken that has, for some reason, been reduced drastically in scale.) She deep-fried them (or maybe 'bake-barbecued' them), applied some hot sauce, and served them on a plate that included some celery from the Anchor Bar's regular antipasto and some of the blue-cheese dressing normally used as the house dressing for salads. If the regulars were puzzled about what to do with the blue-cheese dressing, they were presumably too grateful to say so.

The accounts of Dom and Frank also agree that the wings were an immediate success – famous throughout Buffalo within weeks. In the clipping libraries of the Buffalo newspapers, I could find only one article that dealt with the Bellissimo family and their restaurant in that period – a long piece on Frank and Teressa in the *Courier-Express* in 1969, five years after the invention of the chicken wing. It talks a lot about the musicians who appeared at the Bellissimo's restaurant over the years and about the entertainers who used to drop in after road shows. It mentions the custom Teressa and Frank had in times gone by of offering a few songs themselves late on a Saturday night – Teressa emerging from behind the pasta pots in the kitchen to belt out 'Oh Marie' or

'Tell Me That You Love Me'. It does not mention chicken wings.

Maybe Dom and Frank Bellissimo got fuzzy on dates after some time passed. By chance, my most trusted contemporary observers, the Katzes, were living out of the city during the crucial period; Linda Katz looked surprised to hear that there had ever been a time when people did not eat chicken wings. The exact date of the discovery seemed a small matter, though, compared to the central historical fact that, whatever the circumstances, the first plate of Buffalo chicken wings emerged from the kitchen of the Anchor Bar. It seemed to me that if a pack of revisionist historians descended on Buffalo, itching to get their hands on some piece of conventional wisdom to refute, they would have no serious quarrel with the basic story of how the Buffalo chicken wing was invented – although the feminists among them might point out that the City of Buffalo's proclamation would have been more accurate if it had named as the inventor Teressa Bellissimo. The inventor of the airplane, after all, was not the person who told Wilbur and Orville Wright that it might be nice to have a machine that could fly.

*   *   *

'A blue-collar dish for a blue-collar town', one of the Buffalonians who joined the Katz family and me on our chicken-wing tour said, reminding me that an historian is obligated to put events in the context of their setting, even if his mouth happens to be full at the time. Buffalo does have the reputation of being a blue-collar town – a blue-collar town that during the winter is permanently white with snow. Buffalonians who do much traveling have resigned themselves to the fact that the standard response to hearing that someone comes from Buffalo is a Polish joke or some line like 'Has the snow melted yet?' Buffalo has always had a civic morale problem; one of the T-shirts for sale in town reads 'Buffalo: City of No Illusions'. Now that it is common to be served a dish called 'Buffalo chicken wings' in places like Boston or Atlanta, is the problem being exacerbated by Buffalo's identification with a local specialty made from what is considered to be one of the chicken's less majestic parts? Frank Bellissimo seemed to argue against that interpretation. 'Anybody can sell steak,' he once said. 'But if you sell odds and ends of one thing or another, then you're doing something.' The celebrated visitors who troop through the Anchor Bar are, after all, almost always favorably impressed by Buffalo chicken wings. Craig Claiborne, the renowned food writer for the *New York Times*, proclaimed them 'excellent' in one of his columns – although he may have undercut the compliment a bit by saying in the same paragraph that he had remained in Buffalo for only three hours.

A Buffalo stockbroker named Robert M. Budin once wrote a piece for the *Courier-Express* Sunday magazine suggesting, in a lighthearted way, that the city adopt the chicken wing as its symbol. Budin's piece begins with two Buffalonians discussing what had happened when one of them was at a party in Memphis and was asked by a local where he was from. Deciding to 'take him face on', the visiting Buffalonian had said, 'I'm from Buffalo.' Instead of asking if the snow had melted yet, the local had said, 'Where those dynamite chicken wings come from?'

'You mean positive recognition?' the friend who is hearing the story asks. It becomes obvious to the two of them that Buffalonians should 'mount a campaign to associate Buffalo with chicken wings and rid ourselves of the negatives of snow and cold and the misunderstood beef-on-weck'. Budin suggested that the basketball team be called the Buffalo Wings, that the mayor begin wearing a button that says 'Do Your Thing With Wings', and that a huge statue of a chicken wing (medium hot) be placed in the convention center.

When I telephoned Budin to inquire about the response to his suggestion, he said it had not been overwhelming. He told me, in fact, that he had embarked on a new campaign to improve Buffalo's reputation. Budin said that a lot of people believed that the city's image suffered from its name. I remembered that his Sunday-magazine piece had ended 'Buffalo, thy name is chicken wing'. Surely he was not suggesting that the name of the city be changed to Chicken Wing, New York. No. What should be changed, he told me, was not the name but its pronunciation. He had taken to pronouncing the first syllable as if it were spelled 'boo' – so that Buffalo rhymes with Rue de Veau. 'It has a quality to it that lifts it above the prosaic "Buffalo",' he said.

Maybe. But I suspect that it's only a matter of time before Budin tells some corporate executive in Memphis or Cincinnati that he is calling from Boofalo and the executive says, 'Has the snoo melted yet?'

* * *

On my last evening in Buffalo – just before the Katzes and I drove out on Niagara Falls Boulevard to try the wings at a place called Fat Man's Got 'Em, and just before I got final instructions from Judy Katz about the cardboard bucket of wings I was planning to take back to New York from Santora's the next day, in the way that a medievalist might haul home a small thirteenth-century tapestry ('Get the big bucket. Whatever's left over will be fine the next morning') – I met a man named John Young, who told me, 'I am actually the creator of the wing.' Young, who is black, reminded me that black people have always eaten chicken wings. What he invented, he said, was the sauce that created Buffalo chicken wings – a special concoction he calls mambo sauce. He said that chicken wings in mambo sauce became his specialty in the middle sixties, and that he even registered the name of his restaurant, John Young's Wings 'n Things, at the county courthouse before moving to Illinois in 1970.

'If the Anchor Bar was selling chicken wings, nobody in Buffalo knew it then,' Young said. 'After I left here, everybody started chicken wings.'

Young, who had returned to Buffalo a few months before our talk, told me that those who had copied the dish must be saying, 'Oh, man! The original King of the Wings is back. He's fixin' to do a job on you.' In fact, Young said, he was pleased to see so many people in Buffalo make money off his invention – a magnanimous sentiment that I had also heard expressed by the Bellissimos.

The wings Young invented were not chopped in half – a process he includes in the category of 'tampering with them.' They were served breaded, covered in mambo sauce. It is true, a local poultry distributor told me, that

John Young as well as Frank Bellissimo started buying a lot of chicken wings in the middle sixties, but there was no reason for the distributor to have kept the sales receipts that might indicate who was first. 'First with what?' I thought, as I sampled an order of medium and an order of hot at Santora's while picking up my bucket-to-go. Was the Buffalo chicken wing invented when Teressa Bellissimo thought of splitting it in half and deep-frying it and serving it with celery and blue-cheese dressing? Was it invented when John Young started using mambo sauce and thought of elevating wings into a specialty? How about the black people who have always eaten chicken wings? The way John Young talked, black people may have been eating chicken wings in thirteenth-century Spain. How is it that historians can fix the date of the Battle of Agincourt with such precision? How can they be so certain of its outcome?

First published in *Third Helpings*, 1980

Eating with the Pilgrims

This Thanksgiving, our family was finally able to sit down together and give thanks over a meal of spaghetti carbonara. It has been several years, of course, since I began my campaign to have the national Thanksgiving dish changed from turkey to spaghetti carbonara – I love spaghetti carbonara – but until now invitations to have Thanksgiving dinner at friends' houses prevented our family from practicing what I preached. This year, nobody invited us over for Thanksgiving dinner – my wife's theory being that word got around town that I always make a pest of myself berating the hostess for serving turkey instead of spaghetti carbonara. In my defense, I should say that my daughters do not believe that our lack of invitations has anything at all to do with my insistence on bringing the spaghetti carbonara issue to the attention of the American public at any appropriate opportunity. They believe it may have something to do with my tendency to spill cranberry sauce on my tie.

I'll admit that my campaign might have been inspired partly by my belief that turkey is basically something college dormitories use to punish students for hanging around on Sunday. I'll admit that early in the campaign I brought up some advantages that are only esthetic – the fact, for instance, that the President would not be photographed every year receiving a large platter of spaghetti carbonara from the Eastern Association of Spaghetti Carbonara Growers. As King Vittorio Emmanuelle once said to his Chancellor of the Exchequer, 'Spaghetti doesn't grow on trees.' I'll admit that I would love to see what those masters of the float maker's art at Macy's might come up with as a 300-square-foot depiction of a plate of spaghetti carbonara. I'll admit that I'd find it refreshing to hear sports announcers call some annual tussle the Spaghetti Carbonara Day Classic.

My campaign, though, has been based also on deeper historical and philosophical considerations. Nobody knows if the Pilgrims really ate turkey at the first Thanksgiving dinner. The only thing we know for sure about what the Pilgrims ate is that it couldn't have tasted very good. They were from East Anglia, a part of England whose culinary standards are symbolized by the fact that any number of housewives there are this week serving Brussels sprouts that were put on to boil shortly after the Pilgrims left. Also, it's all very well to say that we should give thanks by eating the meal our forebears ate, but, as it happens, one of the things I give thanks for every year is that those people were not my forebears. Who wants forebears who put people in the stocks for playing the harpsichord on the Sabbath or having an innocent little game of pinch and giggle? In fact, ever since it became fashionable to dwell on the atrocities of American history – ever since, that is, we entered what the historians call The Era of Year-Round Yom Kippur – I have been more and more grateful that none of my forebears got near this place before 1906. When it comes to slavery and massacring Indians and the slaughter of the American buffalo and the assorted scandals of the Spanish–American War, my family's hands are clean. It used to be that an American who wanted to put on airs made claims about how long his family has been here. Now the only people left for a first-generation American to envy are the immigrants who arrived in the last half-dozen years. They don't even have to feel guilty about the Vietnam War.

* * *

Naturally, the whole family went over to Raffeto's pasta store on Houston Street to see the spaghetti cut. It's important, I think, to have these holiday rituals. As the meal began, I asked the children if they had any questions about our forebears.

'Was Uncle Benny responsible for the First World War just because he was already in St. Jo then?' my younger daughter asked.

'Not directly,' I said. 'He didn't have his citizenship.'

'Is it really true that your grandparents got mixed up about American holidays and used to have a big turkey dinner on the Fourth of July and shoot fireworks off in the park on Thanksgiving?' my older daughter asked.

'At least they had nothing to do with snookering the Indians out of Massachusetts,' I said. 'Be thankful for that.'

Then, as is traditional, I told the children the story of the first Thanksgiving:

In England a long time ago, there were people called Pilgrims who were very strict about making sure everyone observed the Sabbath and nobody cooked food with any flavor and that sort of thing, and they decided to go to America where they could enjoy Freedom to Nag. The other people in England said 'Glad to see the back of them,' and put on some Brussels sprouts to boil in case any of their descendants craved a veggie in 1981. In America, the Pilgrims tried farming, but they couldn't get much done because they were always putting each other in the stocks for crimes like Suspicion of Cheerfulness. The Indians took pity on the Pilgrims and helped them with their farming, even though the Indians thought the Pilgrims were about as much fun as a teen-age circumcision. The Pilgrims were so grateful that they invited the Indians over for a Thanksgiving meal, and the Indians, having had some experience with Pilgrim cuisine in the past, took the precaution of bringing along one dish of their own. They brought a dish that their ancestors had learned many generations before from none other than Christopher Columbus, who was known to the Indians as 'the big Italian fella.' The dish was spaghetti carbonara – made with pancetta bacon and fontina and the best imported prosciutto. The Pilgrims hated it. They said it was 'heretically tasty' and 'the work of the devil' and 'the sort of thing foreigners eat.' The Indians were so disgusted that on the way back to their village after dinner one of them made a remark about the Pilgrims that was repeated for generations and unfortunately caused confusion among historians about the first Thanksgiving meal. He said 'What a bunch of turkeys!'

First published in the *Nation*, 12 December 1981

Stalking the Barbecued Mutton

I have wronged the state of Kentucky, but compared to the Kentucky Fried Chicken people I am an innocent. All I did was to pass on the information that a friend of mine named Marshall J. Dodge III – a man renowned on the East Coast for having somehow forged a successful career as a semi-retired amateur folklorist – claimed to have experienced the supreme fried chicken in a town called Rabbit Hash, Kentucky, while touring the area with a calliope restorer of his acquaintance. Local connoisseurs quickly pointed out that Marshall must have been thinking of a chicken restaurant in Cynthiana, Kentucky – Rabbit Hash being a place so small that the goods and services it offers the traveller probably don't extend to premium gasoline. People I know in the state seemed satisfied with my explanation that Marshall is the sort of person who would never say Cynthiana when he could say Rabbit Hash. Not long ago, I thought of making further amends by journeying to Cynthiana and sampling a platter or two of the chicken in question; that sort of penance is one of my specialties. Then a serious eater I know in Covington informed me, in the sort of voice a heavy investor in Mexican savings banks might use to discuss the re-evaluation of the peso, that the Cynthiana restaurant had closed its doors. I was not surprised. In the last several years, legendary fried-chicken places seem to have closed up at about the rate that indoor shopping malls open – Mrs. Stroud's, in Kansas City, and Mrs. Kremer's, near Jefferson City, just to toss off the names of two darkened shrines in my own home state. Because a superior fried-chicken restaurant is often the institutional extension of a single chicken-obsessed woman, I realize that, like a good secondhand bookstore or a bad South American dictatorship, it is not easily passed down intact. Still, in sullen moments I blame these lamentable closings on the agribusiness corporations' vertical integration of the broiler industry. In fact, in sullen moments I blame almost everything on the vertical integration of the broiler industry – the way some people trace practically any sort of mischief or natural disaster back to the Central Intelligence Agency, and some people, presumably slightly more sophisticated, blame everything on the interstate-highway program. If the civilization really is about to crumble, everybody is entitled to his own idea of which is the most significant crack. Which brings us to Kentucky Fried Chicken.

It occurred to me this summer, while I was touring one of the neon-sign displays the Smithsonian mounted in the Bicentennial Year to remind us of the roots of our culture, that Kentucky Fried Chicken is what a schoolboy in Osaka or a housewife in Brussels thinks fried chicken tastes like. The world may be growing smaller, but schoolboys in Osaka have never even heard of Mrs. Stroud. Kentucky Fried Chicken has become the symbol of fast food, even though a chicken fried with care and respect is particularly slow food – pan-frying being a process that requires enough time to make any prospective diner begin worrying about whether he has come close to filling himself up with pickled watermelon rind and assorted relishes. It is also a symbol, I realized, of Kentucky – as if French cuisine were associated in the minds of all foreigners with the sort of frozen French fries dished out to hot-rodders in greasy drive-ins. Are the Swiss thought of as people who sit around all the time eating what high-school dining halls in the Midwest call Swiss steak? The reputation of Kentucky could be reclaimed, I decided, only if the people who spread the word about food were tipped off to a Kentucky specialty that would blot out memories of what Colonel Sanders himself has called 'nothing but a fried dough-ball wrapped around some chicken'. I resolved to seek out the barbecued mutton of western Kentucky – a unique regional delicacy I heard about when a restaurant tout wrote me to say that the motto on the menu of her favorite restaurant in Owensboro said, 'Mary Had a Little Lamb. Won't You Have Some, Too?'

I made this decision in collaboration with Tom Chaney, a loyal son of the state, who lives in Horse Cave. We were eating country ham at the time. I admit that I would rather say Horse Cave than Owensboro, but, as it happens, Chaney really does live in Horse Cave. In fact, his attachment to his home ground is so strong that he has, by his own count, made no fewer than six unsuccessful attempts to leave for good. The place he keeps coming back to is in the south-central part of the state, in a region noted for tobacco and immense limestone caves and, some say, country ham. We were eating the ham in a nearby town called Sulphur Well, in the company of Tom's Aunt Daisie Carter, who spent fifty-one years in the Hart County school system and seems none the worse for wear. The restaurant was a small brick building identified on a Coke sign as Porter's – a place that seems to have inherited the local country-ham trade from the Beula Villa, an old hotel that used to serve as headquarters for people who drank the sulphuric water of the area to clear up whatever seemed to be bothering them. I had sampled the magic spring and, just before we went in to lunch, revealed to Chaney my suspicion that the reputation of Porter's might rest on the fact that anything would taste good after that water. But the ham turned out to be a triumph – sliced thin, and fried, and served with a bowl of redeye gravy. In fact, it occurred to me that country ham rather than barbecued mutton might be the local specialty that could put soggy fried chicken out of the public mind – until Mrs. Carter informed me that the most authentic country hams are illegal.

The actual ham we were wolfing down, she assured me, was quite within the law, but the sort of country ham that local people traditionally bought from a farmer – a farmer who might kill three or four hogs a year, cure the hams to sell, and use the rest of the meat for his own table – could no longer be sold legally because such farmers were obviously not set up to pass modern government inspections.

'You mean you have to buy the country hams you cook at home from a supermarket?' I asked.

'Well, it's sort of like bootleg whiskey,' Mrs. Carter told me, making it clear from her tone that she had not been the kind of schoolteacher who spent her spare time roaming the neighborhood kicking over stills and lecturing on the evils of Demon Rum.

I suddenly had a vision of Tom and his Aunt Daisie racing from their supplier with three or four bootleg hams in the back seat, the Agriculture Department's version of revenuers in hot pursuit – Tom and Aunt Daisie tearing around curves, losing the law at last on the back roads they know so well, and arriving home with the contraband they would cook secretly at night, hoping that the succulent aroma would not draw the authorities to their door. Knowing that people in some parts of Kentucky are still sensitive about their reputation for free-lance distilling, I could hardly draw attention to a product whose most authentic version was illegal. We each had two or three more pieces of ham while we talked it over. Then Tom asked me how the sulphur water had affected my health.

'I feel like a million,' I said. 'A little full, but like a million.'

Tom was reminded of a legendary eater in Horse Cave named Miss Fannie Hiser, a large woman who used to live with his Aunt Minnie. After everybody had finished one of the huge Sunday dinners Miss Fannie prepared, Tom recalled, she used to lean back in her chair, fold her hands contentedly under her ample midsection, and say, 'Thank God for capacity.'

* * *

'Are you sure this place we're going serves decent fried chicken?' I asked Tom late that afternoon. Tom had gathered some barbecued-mutton intelligence from his operatives in western Kentucky, and we decided to go over it while eating a fried-chicken supper with Tom's father, Boots Chaney, a more or less retired insurance man who remains fully active as a chicken eater. What had aroused my suspicion was Tom's choice of the concession restaurant in Mammoth Cave National Park – the sort of restaurant I have been suspicious of since my wife and a friend of ours waited forty-five minutes in a Bryce Canyon version for some broiled brook trout, only to discover when it finally arrived that it had been broiling the entire time.

I was reassured when I noticed that the menu specified native chicken and a thirty-minute wait. 'It's heartening to see that a restaurant in a national park is going to take the time to pan-fry some chicken,' I told Tom. 'It's the sort of thing that could help restore Americans' faith in their government.' A necessary assumption in serving the slow-food variety of fried chicken is that the people waiting for it in the dining room are waiting with people they don't mind waiting with. Waiting for pan-fried chicken with the Chaneys is a treat. They share an office in Horse Cave – a two-room affair they sometimes refer to as Bogus Enterprises, Inc. (Tom Chaney's enterprises include helping run a tobacco-and-corn farm, which he owns in partnership with his Aunt Daisie Carter, and trying to form a professional repertory theatre in Horse Cave; Boots Chaney's enterprises were summed up by some tony-looking stationery his son had made up for him with the legend 'Widows Tended – Lies Told – Whiskey Hauled'.) The Chaneys also share a fondness for anecdotes about the area – particularly about the Cave Wars that took place in the twenties and thirties, when independent cave operators competed for the tourist trade with merchandising devices like blowing up each other's entrances, or stealing the body of Floyd Collins from where it was being displayed in a cave near the one that fatally trapped him in 1925, or outfitting their shills in uniforms that looked official enough to make an unwary tourist think he was being directed to a national park rather than to a free-lance hole in the limestone. No wonder people look so sour as they emerge from fast-food emporiums: they probably haven't heard a good story in years.

* * *

I approached Owensboro warily. Barbecue is a touchy subject all over the country. Except for the universal agreement that the best barbecue of all is served in Kansas City, my home town, there is a lot of regional quibbling on the subject – not just about whose barbecue is best but even about what barbecue is. In the Southwest, for instance, people ordinarily barbecue ribs, but in North Carolina the word is used as a noun referring only to chopped pork that has been flavored, in a manner of speaking, with a vinegar-based sauce. It is normal for regional loyalists to be both chauvinistic and arcane when talking about the local version. A traveller who returns to, say, New York from a trip to North Carolina and reports to North Carolina expatriates there that the barbecue didn't seem to amount to much subjects himself to stern geographical probing:

'Were you east of Rocky Mount?'

'Is Goldsboro east of Rocky Mount?'

'West. There's no decent barbecue west of Rocky Mount.'

'I don't know where Rocky Mount is, but it must be east of all the towns I ate barbecue in.'

'I expect so.'

Although I assumed that people in Owensboro would be proud of their local version – not just a different sort of pork or a different sauce formula or a different way of slicing beef but an entirely different animal – it also occurred to me that Owensboro might not want to be proclaimed the Barbecued-Mutton Capital of the World. It's a fairly sophisticated city, after all, with four distilleries, and a General Electric plant that was turning out more than half a million tubes a day before it was struck low by the Japanese transistor, and two colleges, and a river port on the Ohio, and a thirteen-story motel just as perfectly round as a good silo. Baffling as it may seem, there are residents of Cincinnati who are not pleased when I refer to their city as the Center of Greek Chili in Ohio. There was also the possibility that Owensboro already had a slogan that it would be reluctant to part with.

'No, I think slogans for cities are trite,' the executive vice-president of the Chamber of Commerce told me. 'We don't have one anymore.'

'What did the slogan use to be?'

'Opportunity Center of the U.S.A.'

'I see what you mean. But you do think that Owensboro is – in fact, if not in slogan – the barbecued-mutton capital of the world?'

'Undoubtedly,' he said.

Two hours later, Tom Chaney, who had been doing some further consultation with a specialist from Union County, informed me by telephone that Waverly, Kentucky, forty-five miles west of Owensboro, might be the barbecued-mutton capital of the world. Not an hour after that, the proprietor of Posh & Pat's, a barbecue place in Henderson, on the way to Waverly, said of Owensboro, 'They've got the reputation, we've got the barbecue.' Meanwhile, I had been told that the premier barbecued mutton was served by a man named Woolfolk in Cairo, Kentucky, just south of Henderson, but only in the summer. I knew I had come to the right territory.

* * *

'How come this is the only area where mutton is barbecued?' I asked an Owensboro merchant who had been kind enough to give me change for a nickel parking meter.

'I expect because there are so many Catholics here,' he said.

I didn't want to appear ignorant. 'Yeah,' I said, 'I suppose that'd do it.'

As I was searching my mind for some connection between the Roman rite and mutton consumption, the merchant told me that the large Catholic churches in town have always staged huge picnics that feature barbecue and burgoo – burgoo, another staple of Owensboro barbecue restaurants, being a soupy stew that I, for some reason, had always associated with southern Illinois. In the early days, the church picnics apparently served barbecued goat. In fact, Owensboro might have arrived at barbecued mutton by a process of elimination, since people in the area seem willing to barbecue just about any extant mammal. In western Kentucky, barbecue restaurants normally do 'custom cooking' for patrons who have the meat but not the pit, and among the animals that Posh & Pat's offers to barbecue is raccoon. The Shady Rest, one of the most distinguished barbecue joints in Owensboro, has a sign that says 'If It Will Fit on the Pit, We Will Barbecue It.' It is probably fortunate that the people of the area settled on barbecued mutton as the local delicacy before they had a go at beaver or polecat.

* * *

After only six or eight meals of barbecued mutton, I had prepared the report I would give to the first internationally influential eater I ran across. 'They serve it just about every way,' I would say. 'Sliced, chopped, ribs, hidden in burgoo.'

'Is it good?'

'It's not bad at all.'

'Just not bad?'

'I believe I prefer it to Greek Chili,' I would say. 'Also, as far as I know, it is not illegal in its most authentic form.' Barbecued mutton is, as the saying goes, not Kansas City, but there were reasons not to apply such standards. In Posh & Pat's, after all, the restaurant gossip going on when I walked in was not about someone's secret sauce formula but about the Burger Farm franchise just down the interstate being replaced by a Wiener King. A local restaurant man who happened to be at

Posh & Pat's counter downing a sliced-mutton sandwich said he was thinking of opening a new steak restaurant with an 'old depot' décor. 'It's all Western or Barn here now,' he told me. With the franchisers and décor-mongers closing in, any authentic local specialty obviously needs celebrating. Did I want a nice river city like Owensboro – a city that, according to my calculations, has a barbecued-mutton restaurant for every fifty-one hundred and eighty-eight residents – to be known as the Ex-Tube Capital of the World? Was it fair to serious eaters like the Chaneys that foreigners should believe their state to be nothing but a jungle of fast-food franchises? 'Kentucky is the Barbecued-Mutton Capital of the World,' I would tell the first eater of influence I could find. 'Spread the word.'

First published in the *New Yorker*, 7 February 1977

Just Try It

What I decided to tell Sarah about catfish was that it tastes like flounder. She eats flounder, although I can't say she's an enthusiast. When it comes to food, her enthusiasm runs toward chocolate – her favorite dish (if that's the word) being a chocolate-chocolate-chip-ice-cream cone with chocolate sprinkles. She once went in the Village Halloween Parade as a chocolate-chocolate-chip-ice-cream cone with chocolate sprinkles – the ultimate tribute. I can't remember what I told her flounder tastes like. Whatever it was must have been mentioned in a speech of considerable eloquence. There is general agreement in our family that my speeches on how closely Chinese fried dumplings resemble ravioli were as persuasive as any I have delivered – Sarah happens to love ravioli; I wouldn't be at all surprised to see her suit up as a ravioli some Halloween – but four years of such speeches were required before Sarah agreed to take one microbite of one dumpling. Trying to persuade Sarah to taste something is not a struggle that is undertaken in the expectation that success will be rewarded with the opportunity to see her yelp with joy as she cleans her plate. She's not likely to be crazy about it. Once my wife, Alice, used a food processor and creamed cheese and absolutely fresh spinach and considerable imagination to turn out a spinach dish one bite of which would have probably caused Paul Bocuse to ask about the possibility of apprenticing for a while in Alice's kitchen. Sarah tasted the spinach and, displaying a certain sensitivity toward the feelings of the chef, said, 'It's better than a carrot.' I must admit that the chef and I have found that phrase useful ever since. As we walk out of a movie, one of us sometimes says, 'Well, it was better than a carrot' or, occasionally, 'That one was not quite as good as a carrot.'

The notion that Sarah might be persuaded to taste catfish was based on my observation that, at ten, she might have been growing slightly more adventuresome about nonchocolate foodstuffs. The days are past when she refused to go to Chinatown unless she was carrying a bagel ('just in case'), and even though she still doesn't eat salad, she is too old to repeat her grand preschool gesture of refusing to return to a summer-recreation program because those in charge had the gall to serve her salad at snack time. ('They gave me salad!' she said, in the tone a countess who'd been roughly handled by customs inspectors might have said, 'They searched my gown!') Slowly, arbitrarily, she has expanded to half a dozen or so the exotic dishes she enjoys in apparent contradiction to her entire policy on eating – so that she will casually down, for instance, a Chinese dish called beef with baby clam sauce, like a teetotaler who happens to make an exception for slivovitz or south-Georgia busthead. Still, I often hear myself making the sort of appeal I can imagine thousands of parents making to thousands of ten-year-olds at the same time: 'Just try it. Would I lie to you about something as important to me as fried dumplings? If you don't like it, you don't have to eat it. Just try it.'

There are, of course, a lot of grown-ups who won't try catfish. Some people think catfish are ugly. To be perfectly honest about it, just about everybody thinks catfish are ugly. I have run into people willing to defend the looks of hyenas and wild boars, but I have never heard anyone say, 'The catfish, in its own way, is really quite beautiful.' A catfish has whiskers that might look all right if attached to some completely different animal – although an appropriate animal does not come immediately to mind. The best thing that can be said of a catfish's skin is that it is removed before eating. At a fish plant, anyone who cleans catfish is ordinarily called a catfish skinner; part of the process is to pull off the skin with the kind of pliers that are used by other people to snip the heads off roofing nails. People who are particularly conscious of the tendency of catfish to feed along muddy river bottoms think of cleaning a catfish as a process that has ultimate failure built right into it; they avoid catfish precisely because they believe that there is no such thing as a clean catfish. Some people avoid catfish because they believe that no catfish – even one whose bones have been removed by a boner with the skill of a surgeon – is harboring fewer than seven small bones somewhere within it. There are also people who wouldn't think of trying a fish that in some parts of the country is thought to be eaten mainly by poor folks. In the South, where most catfish is consumed, even the way restaurants customarily advertise it implies that they are offering a bargain rather than a delicacy – 'CATFISH AND

HUSHPUPPIES, ALL YOU CAN EAT: $3.25'. Writing in the *New York Times* once about the place of catfish in his Mississippi boyhood, Craig Claiborne did describe the pleasure of eating it on summer picnics that included ladies carrying parasols, but he also left the impression that catfish was eaten on picnics because his mother wouldn't allow it inside her house.

With catfish farming now a considerable industry in Mississippi and Arkansas and Alabama, there has been some effort in recent years to make catfish a respectable national dish, rather than a slightly disreputable regional specialty, but seeing it on the menu of the sort of eclectic Manhattan restaurant that also serves salmon mousse and fettuccine with wild mushrooms still leaves the impression of having run into a stock-car racer at a cro-quet match. I preferred to think, of course, that the class implications of catfish eating would have no effect on Sarah's willingness to try it out – we have tried to raise her to believe that honest pan-fried chicken is in no way inferior to pâté – but it is impossible to predict such things; she happens to love particularly expensive cuts of smoked salmon, and the first wild-card dish she doted on in Chinatown was roast squab.

Naturally, I am interested in any opportunity to nudge Sarah's eating habits in a democratic direction, and that was one reason I chose the Fourth Annual St. Johns River Catfish Festival in Crescent City, Florida, as the destin-ation for a little trip we were planning to take together while the rest of the family was occupied elsewhere. The other reason was that I happen to love catfish. I even love hushpuppies. Sarah was enthusiastic about going to

Florida, although I must admit that the first question she asked was how far Crescent City is from Disney World. Then she narrowed her eyes and said, 'Catfish?'

'It tastes like flounder,' I said. 'You can just try it.'

'OK,' she said, in the voice she uses for acknowledging the necessity of wearing gloves on cold days. 'Maybe.'

'Their other specialty is alligator tail,' I said. 'And for all I know alligator tail may taste like flounder, too.'

Sarah didn't bother to reply to that one.

* * *

'I might try some catfish,' Sarah said on the day before the festival, as we were discussing preparations with its founder, Ronnie Hughes. 'It depends on how it looks.'

'If you don't have any before the catfish-skinning contest, I suspect you won't have any after,' Hughes said.

It was clear by then that the people in Crescent City, a pleasant little north-Florida town below Jacksonville, were not among those trying to tidy up the reputation of the catfish. When Hughes, the publisher of the *Crescent City Courier-Journal* and *Trading Post Shopper*, persuaded the Rotary Club to sponsor a catfish festival, it was partly with the idea of celebrating the local commercial catfishing industry, but there has never been any claim that what the fishermen catch is anything other than an ugly beast with more bones than any fish has need of. 'It's not something that's going to grace a table,' Hughes said. Among the articles in his newspaper's Catfish Festival supplement was one that investigated the various styles of trying to eat a catfish – styles that divided catfish eaters into pickers, peelers, chompers, suckers, spitters, and animals – and concluded that all of them were more or less unsuccessful. In other parts of the South, boosters of the domestic catfish industry may argue for wider acceptance of their product on the ground that farm-raised catfish do not have a muddy taste; a resident of Crescent City tends to say he prefers the wild catfish caught in the nearby St. Johns River precisely because they do taste muddy. People around Crescent City take the catfish on its own terms.

'We don't mind if you refer to Crescent City and southern Putnam County as "the sticks" or "red-neck country",' the brochure that the Rotary put out for the Catfish Festival said. 'We're a down-home community.' In north Florida, it is common to hear people speak of their part of the state as 'the real Florida' – meaning that it is the part still not dominated by tourists or retired Yankees or Cubans or anybody else except people who like to refer to themselves as crackers. 'This here's a natural Florida cracker here,' is the way Buck Buckles, the man who always presides over the preparation of the festival's swamp cabbage, was introduced to Sarah and me. The celebration of crackers in southern Putnam County is for qualities pretty much like those attached to the catfish – being ornery and plain and uncouth and unconcerned about offending the pompous ('He don't care,' Gamble Rogers, a country storyteller who performed at the festival, said of a cracker fisherman in one of his stories who rams the boats of tourists. 'He flat do not care') and basically lovable.

Being down-home, people in Crescent City would

not think of calling swamp cabbage by its other name – hearts of palm. They sometimes refer to another local specialty, soft-shelled turtle, as 'cooter'. Buck Buckles, whose crew helps him gather four hundred Sabal palm trees every year from an area scheduled for clear-cutting, is aware that some people serve hearts of palm fresh in salad, but for the Catfish Festival he cooks swamp cabbage for a day or so with noodles and salted bacon.

'How did you happen to learn how to do all that?' I asked Buckles, a friendly man in his sixties who has worked most of his life as a heavy-equipment contractor.

'Ever hear of Hoover?' Buckles said. There wasn't much money around southern Putnam County in the thirties, he told me, and anyone who wanted something to eat often had to 'catch it, tree it, cut it out of a palm, or scratch it out of a hole.'

Sarah was impressed with the process of preparing swamp cabbage – cutting the trunk of the palm into logs and then using machetes to strip away one layer after another in order to reach the heart. She announced, though, that she wasn't going to try any. I hadn't expected her to. The name 'swamp cabbage' didn't seem to bother her, but she never eats anything that might ever be part of a salad – just to be on the safe side.

I also hadn't expected her to try the sort of exotic meats that Satsuma Gardens, a restaurant ten miles up the road from Crescent City, includes in what its menu lists as a 'Swamp Critter Special' – frogs' legs, soft-shelled turtle, and gator tail. I was eager to taste gator tail myself – partly because it is the only exotic meat I have ever run across that nobody seems to describe as tasting like chicken. I suppose I harbored some faint hope that somebody might interest Sarah by saying that it tastes a bit like roast squab – as it turned out, most people in Putnam County compare gator tail to pork chops – but after we had a talk about alligators with John Norris, one of the proprietors of the St. Johns Crab Company, that hope evaporated. The St. Johns Crab Company is a few miles from Satsuma, in Welaka, where there are a number of fish plants that buy the crabs and catfish that the same families have been hauling out of the St. Johns for generations. The company provides a lot of the catfish eaten at the festival, although the impossibility of diverting four tons of small catfish – the kind Southerners like to eat – from regular customers once a year means that the festival supply is quietly supplemented by some farm-raised catfish from Mississippi, with the hope that festival-goers will not be able to detect that telltale lack of mud.

'They don't just take a whole alligator tail and serve it like that,' Norris said, in a reassuring way. 'They cut out the muscle – '

'Well,' I said, in the tone of someone who has been reassured, 'once they dispose of that, then – '

'That's the part you eat,' Norris said.

As it turned out, I liked gator tail – at least the way it was prepared by Jack Ketter at the Satsuma Gardens, a friendly little roadside restaurant that is decorated with a beer-can collection and signs with sayings like 'A Woman with Horse Sense Never Becomes a Nag'. The first time I tasted alligator – at a vast, crowded restaurant where the meal reminded me once again that any time you're called to your table over a loudspeaker, what you are served there is likely to be disappointing – I found it rather, well, muscular. Ketter, though, serves a first-rate gator tail – cut into thin slices, pounded, and lightly fried. In fact, he caters the gator-tail booth at the festival, since alligator can be served only by a restaurant proprietor licensed to buy meat from the supply acquired by the shooting of 'nuisance gators' that have been declared an exception to the alligator-protection law because of a tendency to frighten golfers or snack on Airedales. 'It tastes like veal scallopini,' I said to Sarah during our second meal at Satsuma Gardens. The remark did not inspire Sarah to pick up her fork for a taste. She doesn't eat veal scallopini.

'I might have tried alligator if that man hadn't told us about the muscle,' she said, glancing at my dinner of alligator, catfish, soft-shell crab, fried mushrooms, fried okra, and coleslaw. As it was, she was having a hamburger – which is what she had eaten for lunch at Satsuma Gardens the previous day. 'This place actually has very good hamburgers,' she said. 'In fact, excellent.' At our first Satsuma Gardens meal, the waitress who brought Sarah a sack of potato chips as a side dish (if that's the word) opened the sack as she placed it on the table, and I, remembering that some particularly sophisticated people trace their worldliness to having been taken as children to restaurants by fathers who advised them on selecting the wine and dealing with the captain, looked at the open sack and said, 'That's the way you can tell a classy joint.'

* * *

The Fourth Annual St. Johns River Catfish Festival was held in the Crescent City town park – a long, square block in an area dominated by huge live oaks with Spanish moss. Sarah liked it. She liked the arts-and-crafts booths, particularly the booth that displayed a talking parrot. She liked the parade, which featured a series of Shriners driving by in every conceivable sort of vehicle that a grown man could look silly driving. She was impressed by Geetsie Crosby, the lady who always presides over the catfish chowder at the festival: Mrs. Crosby told Sarah that her own daughter would eat nothing but canned tuna for most of her childhood, and managed to grow up to be a very fine doctor.

'Maybe one of these years we can find a canned-tuna festival,' I said. I had the feeling that Sarah wasn't going to eat much catfish. She had seemed to be preparing me for that on the way to the festival when she said she wasn't really all that hungry. When lunchtime came, I got one catfish dinner instead of two, and offered her a bite.

'I don't really think I want any, thanks,' Sarah said.

'But it tastes like flounder,' I said.

'Does it taste like chocolate?' she said.

I didn't think I could make a very good case for its tasting like chocolate. I hadn't really expected the question. 'Well, at least that leaves us free to go over and watch the catfish-skinning contest,' I said. 'As soon as I finish eating.'

First published in *Third Helpings*, 1980

Talk About Ugly

July 9, 1990

So there I was, butchering a monkfish. As everyone knows, a monkfish is the ugliest creature God ever made.

I realize that those are fighting words among connoisseurs of the drastically unattractive. There are, for instance, people who sincerely believe that a catfish has got all other fish beat for ugliness. I'm here to tell you that compared to a monkfish the average catfish looks like Robert Redford.

In the Pacific Northwest there are people who think that the ugliest creature around is the giant clam they have out there called the geoduck. It's pronounced as if it were spelled gooeyduck, which adds to its unpleasant impression – although, as it happens, gooeyness is one of the few unattractive characteristics it doesn't possess. I won't try to tell you a geoduck is handsome. Its most striking feature is a clam neck that seems to be about the size of a baby elephant's trunk. Still, if I had to describe the appearance of a geoduck in a couple of words, I'd say 'moderately disgusting'. That's a long way from ugliness at the monkfish level.

The monkfish is also known by such names as goosefish, angler, and bellyfish. Calling it something else doesn't help. Its appearance still brings to mind that fine old American phrase, too little heard these days: 'hit upside the head with an ugly stick'.

The head, as it happens, is the ugliest part of a monk-fish. It is huge – a lot bigger than the body. It is shaped sort of like a football that has been sideswiped by a Pontiac station wagon. It has, in the words of a fisherman I know, 'all kinds of doodads hanging off it'. In Nova Scotia, which is where I come in contact with monkfish, fishermen cut the heads off while still at sea. The stated reason for disposing of the head is that the fish plant won't buy it, since nobody has ever figured out a use for a monkfish head. (It doesn't keep long enough to be employed as a device you can threaten to show children if they don't quit fighting over the Nintendo.) I've never been able to escape the feeling, though, that fishermen cut off the head because they don't want anything that ugly on their boat. It makes them shiver.

If you were thinking that without the head a monkfish compares in pure natural beauty to, say, a snow leopard, forget it. The rest of a monkfish is plenty ugly. There is a skin that, by rights, ought to be on a geoduck or something that sounds equally gooey. Instead of the sort of bone structure a respectable fish has, the monkfish has something that reminds most people of a beef bone – although not in a way that makes them long for the open range. Covering the meat on either side of the bone there is a sort of membrane. Is the membrane disgusting? Try hard to think of a membrane you've really liked.

So there I was, butchering a monkfish. Why? Because in our part of Nova Scotia buying an unbutchered monk-fish off a fishing boat is the only way you can get a monkfish, and monkfish, like catfish and geoducks, are absolutely delicious. Also, because I have always harbored a secret desire to have people say of me, 'He's the sort of guy who can butcher a monkfish.' If they did say that, of course, it might be misleading; I don't actually do many other things that are like butchering a monkfish. On the other hand, let's face it: how many things are there that are like butchering a monkfish? Don't forget the membrane.

Removing the membrane is my least favorite part of butchering a monkfish, although, as a veterinarian I know always says about ministering to a cow that has a badly upset stomach, 'There's nothing about it that reminds me a whole lot of opening presents on Christmas morning.' I keep thinking that there's some sort of membrane-removal shortcut I don't know about. I always listen to the noon radio show they have for farmers and fishermen in the hope that someday I'll hear some home economist say something like, 'To get the pesky membrane off a monkfish, simply bury the fish in cornflakes for fifteen or twenty minutes, then wipe briskly with a dry cloth.' So far, nobody on the show has discussed monkfish. Probably too ugly.

So there I am, with the membrane and the gooey skin and the beef bone. What am I thinking? Sometimes I'm thinking, 'Well, at least it doesn't have the head on.' Sometimes I'm thinking, 'Don't forget how good this is going to taste.' When none of that does any good, I'm thinking, 'You're the sort of guy who can butcher a monkfish.'

First published in *Too Soon to Tell*, 1990

Missing Links

Of all the things I've eaten in the Cajun parishes of Louisiana – an array of foodstuffs which has been characterized as somewhere between extensive and deplorable – I yearn most often for boudin. When people in Breaux Bridge or Opelousas or Jeanerette talk about boudin (pronounced 'boo-DAN'), they mean a soft, spicy mixture of rice and pork and liver and seasoning which is squeezed hot into the mouth from a sausage casing, usually in the parking lot of a grocery store and preferably while leaning against a pickup. ('Boudin' means blood sausage to the French, most of whom would probably line up for immigration visas if they ever tasted the Cajun version.) I figure that about eighty per cent of the boudin purchased in Louisiana is consumed before the purchaser has left the parking lot, and most of the rest of it is polished off in the car. In other words, Cajun boudin not only doesn't get outside the state; it usually doesn't even get home. For Americans who haven't been to South Louisiana, boudin remains as foreign as *gado-gado* or *cheb*; for them, the word 'Cajun' on a menu is simply a synonym for burnt fish or too much pepper. When I am daydreaming of boudin, it sometimes occurs to me that of all the indignities the Acadians of Louisiana have had visited upon them – being booted out of Nova Scotia, being ridiculed as rubes and swamp rats by neighboring Anglophones for a couple of centuries, being punished for speaking their own language in the schoolyard – nothing has been as deeply insulting as what restaurants outside South Louisiana present as Cajun food.

The scarcity of boudin in the rest of the country makes it all the more pleasurable to have a Louisiana friend who likes to travel and occasionally carries along an ice chest full of local ingredients, just in case. I happen to have such a friend in James Edmunds, of New Iberia, Louisiana. Over the past twenty years or so, James's visits to New York have regularly included the ritualistic unpacking of an ice chest on my kitchen table. His custom has been to bring the ice chest if he plans to cook a meal during the visit – crawfish étouffée, for instance, or gumbo or his signature shrimp stew. On those trips, the ice chest would also hold some boudin. I was so eager to get my hands on the boudin that I often ate it right in the kitchen, as soon as we heated it through, rather than trying to make the experience more authentic by searching for something appropriate to lean against. In lower Manhattan, after all, it could take a while to find a pickup truck.

Then there came the day when I was sentenced to what I think of as medium-security cholesterol prison. (Once the cholesterol penal system was concessioned out to the manufacturers of statin drugs, medium-security cholesterol prison came to mean that the inmate could eat the occasional bit of bacon from the plate of a generous luncheon companion but could not order his own B.L.T.) James stopped bringing boudin, the warders

having summarily dismissed my argument that the kind
I particularly like – Cajun boudin varies greatly from
maker to maker – was mostly just rice anyway.

I did not despair. James is inventive, and he's flexible.
Several years ago, he decided that an architect friend of
his who lives just outside New Iberia made the best
crawfish étouffée in the area, and, like one of those
research-and-development hot shots who are always
interested in ways of improving the product, he took the
trouble to look into the recipe, which had been handed
down to the architect by forebears of unadulterated
Cajunness. James was prepared for the possibility that
one of the secret ingredients of the architect's blissful
étouffée was, say, some herb available only at certain
times of year in the swamps of the Atchafalaya Basin
Spillway. As it turned out, one of the secret ingredients
was Campbell's cream-of-mushroom soup. (Although
crawfish étouffée, which means smothered crawfish, is
one of the best-known Cajun dishes, it emerged only
in the fifties, when a lot of people assumed that just
about any recipe was enhanced by a can of Campbell's
cream-of-mushroom soup.) During ensuing étouffée
preparations in New York, there would come a moment
when James said, in his soft South Louisiana accent, 'I
think this might be a good time for certain sensitive
people to leave the kitchen for just a little while.' Then
we'd hear the whine of the can opener, followed by an
unmistakable *glub-glub-glub*.

A few years after my sentence was imposed, James
and I were talking on the telephone about an imminent
New York visit that was to include the preparation of

one of his dinner specialties, and he told me not to worry about the problem of items rattling around in his ice chest. I told him that I actually hadn't given that problem much thought, what with global warming and nuclear proliferation and all. As if he hadn't heard me, he went on to say that he'd stopped the rattling with what he called packing-boudin.

'Packing-boudin?'

'That's right,' James said.

I thought about that for a moment or two. 'Well, it's got bubble wrap beat,' I finally said. 'And we wouldn't have to worry about adding to this country's solid-waste-disposal problem. Except for the casing.' The habit of tossing aside the casing of a spent link of boudin is so ingrained in some parts of Louisiana that there is a bumper sticker reading 'Caution: Driver Eating Boudin' – a way of warning the cars that follow about the possibility of their windshields being splattered with what appear to be odd-looking insects. From that visit on, I took charge of packing-boudin disposal whenever James was carrying his ice chest, and I tried not to dwell on my disappointment when he wasn't.

Not long ago, I got a call from James before a business trip to New York which was not scheduled to include the preparation of a Louisiana meal – that is, a trip that would ordinarily not include boudin. He asked if he could store a turducken in my freezer for a couple of days; he was making a delivery for a friend. I hesitated. I was trying to remember precisely what a turducken is, other than something Cajuns make that seems to go against the laws of nature.

James, perhaps thinking that my hesitancy reflected some reluctance to take on the storage job, said, 'There'd be rental-boudin involved, of course.'

'Fair's fair,' I said.

* * *

What led to my being in Louisiana a couple of weeks later for something that James insisted on calling a boudin blitzkrieg is rather complicated. As a matter of convenience, James had picked up the rental-boudin at the same place he'd bought the turducken, Hebert's Specialty Meats, in Maurice, Louisiana. Hebert's is a leading purveyor of turducken, which it makes by taking the bones out of a chicken and a duck and a turkey, stuffing the chicken with stuffing, stuffing the stuffed chicken into a similarly stuffed duck, and stuffing all that, along with a third kind of stuffing, into the turkey. The result cannot be criticized for lacking complexity, and it presents a challenge to the holiday carver almost precisely as daunting as meat loaf.

The emergence of turducken, eight or ten years ago, did not surprise Cajuns. When it comes to eating, they take improvisation for granted. Some people in New Iberia, for instance, collect the sludge left over from mashing peppers at the McIlhenny Tabasco plant and use it to spice up the huge pots of water they employ to boil crawfish. When Thanksgiving approaches, they fill the same huge pots with five or six gallons of lard instead of water and produce deep fried turkey – a dish that is related to the traditional roast turkey in the way that *soupe au pistou* in Provence or *ribollita* in Tuscany is related to the vegetable soup that was served in your high-school cafeteria. James's wife, Susan Hester, who works at the Iberia Parish Library, once heard a deputy sheriff who was lecturing on personal defense recommend buying water-based rather than oil-based pepper spray not only because it comes off the clothing easier but because it is preferable for flavoring the meat being grilled at a cookout.

Although I didn't want to appear ungrateful for the rental-boudin, I reminded James that his buying boudin in Maurice, which is more than twenty miles from New Iberia, flies in the face of the rule promulgated by his old friend Barry Jean Ancelet, a folklorist and French professor at the University of Louisiana at Lafayette: in the Cajun country of Louisiana, the best boudin is always the boudin closest to where you live, and the best place to eat boiled crawfish is always extraordinarily inconvenient to your house. James is aware that this theory has a problem with internal consistency – it means, for instance, that for him the best boudin is at Bonin's meat market, in New Iberia, and for Barry Jean Ancelet it's at The Best Stop Supermarket, in Scott – but he reconciles that by saying that Barry, being a folklorist, has a different notion of objective truth than some other people.

We had never talked much about the source of the boudin James brought to New York, except that I knew it had changed once, some years ago, when a purveyor named Dud Breaux retired. Once his purchase of boudin in Maurice raised the subject, though, James assured me that under ordinary circumstances he follows the Ancelet Dictum: before leaving for New York, he stocks up at Bonin's, assuming that the proprietor happens to be in what James called 'a period of non-retirement'. The proprietor's name is Waldo Bonin, but he is known in New Iberia as Nook. He is a magisterial man with white hair and a white mustache and a white T-shirt and a white apron. Nook Bonin has not retired as many times as Frank Sinatra did, but he is about even with Michael Jordan.

Like one of those boxers who bid farewell to the ring with some regularity, Bonin comes back every time with a little less in his repertoire. For nearly fifty years, he and his wife, Delores, ran a full-service meat market that also included a lot of Cajun specialties. The first time they came out of retirement, they had dropped everything but boudin and cracklins (crunchy pieces of fatback that are produced by rendering lard from a hog) and hogs-head cheese, plus soft drinks for those who weren't going to make it back to their cars with their purchases intact. The second time, when the Bonins started appearing only on Friday afternoons and Saturday mornings, they had dropped the cracklins. As a matter of policy, James doesn't actually eat cracklins – 'I just think it's good to know that there's a line out there you're not going to cross,' he has said – but, as someone who depends on Nook Bonin's boudin, he had to be disturbed by what appeared to be a trend. 'I wouldn't mind losing the Cokes,' he has said, when envisioning what might be dropped in the Bonins' next comeback. 'But it is getting kind of scary.'

The recipe for the boudin sold at Bonin's is a secret. In fact, it has occurred to James that the proprietor himself may not know the secret: people customarily speak of Nook Bonin's boudin, but it is actually made by Delores Bonin, who goes heavy on the rice and uses an array of spices that, I would be prepared to testify under oath, owe nothing to the test kitchens of the Campbell's Soup Company. Although the Bonins have two daughters, neither of them chose to go into the family business. Anna is an administrator in a special-education program, and Melissa is an artist. James and Susan happen to be long-time admirers of Melissa's work – some years ago, they bought the first painting she ever sold – but James can't help thinking that if she had chosen to put her creative energies into boudin-making rather than art, the community would not now be beset by the tension brought on by her parents' stairstep retirements. At this point, James and Susan have pinned their hopes on the Bonins' only grandchild – Melissa's son, Emile. Unfortunately, Emile is only ten years old. James was cheered, though, when we walked into the Bonins' store on a Saturday morning and Delores Bonin reached over the meat case to hand us a photograph of Emile posing behind the device that stuffs boudin into sausage casing. Emile was smiling.

Even assuming that Emile decides to cast his lot with boudin, though, it will be a number of years before he's old enough to take over the business. James and I discussed that situation in the sort of conversation I can imagine a working team from State and Defense having about whether sufficient steps have been taken to guarantee that this country maintains a secure and unbroken supply of cobalt in the face of any contingency. We decided that, just in case the Bonin family line of succession does get broken, I should sample some of the possibilities for what I suppose you'd have to call replacement-boudin. This is why Susan, who was carrying a cutting board and a kitchen knife, and James and I were driving around on a sunny weekend, tasting what Nook Bonin had to offer and testing out, in a judicious way, the work of other purveyors. At least, that's what I would tell the penal authorities if the question ever came up.

*   *   *

By Sunday night, we had tried the boudin from, among other places, Legnon's Boucherie, in New Iberia, and Bruce's U-Need-A-Butcher, in Lafayette, and Poche's Meat Market and Restaurant, in Poche Bridge, and Heleaux's Grocery, also in Lafayette, and, of course, The Best Stop, in Scott. We hadn't by any measure exhausted the supply of even highly recommended boudin purveyors. For instance, we hadn't tried Johnson's Grocery, in Eunice, or Billeaud's, in Broussard, a town near Lafayette that used to have an annual boudin festival. A friend of mine in New Orleans, Randy Fertel, after tracking down the source of the boudin that he looks forward to eating every year at the New Orleans Jazz Fest, had recommended Abe's Cajun Market, in Lake Charles, which is practically in Texas, but there hadn't been time. Still, I had tasted enough contenders for replacement-boudin to tell James that I hoped Nook and Delores Bonin truly understood that for people who have been active all their lives retirement can be a trap.

I had to admit to Barry Jean Ancelet, who joined us at

The Best Stop, that his local purveyor makes a distin-guished link of boudin – moderate, shading toward meaty, when it comes to the all-important rice/meat ratio. Lawrence Menard, who opened The Best Stop in 1986, told us that he now sells between sixty-five hun-dred and seven thousand pounds of boudin a week. In a conversation that began, appropriately, at The Best Stop and continued later that evening in a restaurant called Bubba Frey's, Barry explained the Ancelet Dictum to us in more detail. A link of boudin, he said, is a clean food, essentially treated by Cajuns as 'an enclosed lunch'; it's even cleaner if you eat the casing, which Lawrence Menard himself always does. Boiled crawfish, on the other hand, is notoriously messy, leaving a table piled with shells and crawfish heads. It stands to reason that you'd want to leave that kind of mess far from your lair. He pointed out that for boiled crawfish he and James both favor a place called Hawk's, whose location is inconvenient to both of them and to practically every-body else. In a book called *Cajun Country Guide*, Macon Fry and Julie Posner wrote that the reason Hawk's is so good is that Hawk Arceneaux puts his crawfish through a twenty-four-hour freshwater purging process, but, then again, they're not folklorists.

Since the 'e' in Frey is silent, Bubba Frey's sounds at first like a succinct description of Southern cooking rather than a restaurant. It is a restaurant, though – a bright, knotty-pine place with a Cajun combo that, on the night we were there, included Bubba Frey himself as one of its fiddlers. We went there after a performance of 'Rendezvous des Cadiens', a Cajun radio show that Barry m.c.s every Saturday at the Liberty Theatre in Eunice – a town in an area known as the Cajun Prairies. For some time, Bubba Frey has run a general store in a nearby hamlet called Mowata – a name I don't intend to investigate, just in case it is unconnected with a flood or the discovery of a particularly capacious well – and not long ago he decided to add a restaurant next door. Boudin balls were listed as an appetizer. Boudin isn't commonly served by restaurants, although Café des Amis, in Breaux Bridge, offers something called *oreille de cochon* – beignet dough that is baked in the shape of pigs' ears, covered with powdered sugar, and, for an extra dollar, stuffed with boudin. It's a dollar well spent.

Boudin balls are made by rolling boudin into balls, coating them with something like Zatarain's Fish Fry, and frying away. At Bubba Frey's, they were delicious, and the proprietor, who came over to our table between sets, told us that the boudin was made at his store next door. I told James that the next time he happened to be on the Cajun Prairies he might consider finding out what Bubba's boudin tasted like unfried. Then it occurred to me that if James liked it better than he liked Nook Bonin's boudin he might feel obligated to move to Mowata. James did not seem enthusiastic about that prospect. He and Susan have both lived in New Iberia virtually all their lives, and have a lot of friends there. Also, James subscribes to the theory that, perhaps because the French settlement of the Cajun Prairies included a strong admixture of Germans, people there are a bit stiffer than the people who live in the Cajun bayous. I don't know how stiffness in Cajuns would manifest itself. Maybe they use only two kinds of stuffing in their turduckens.

*   *   *

A couple of weeks later, I heard from James: the boudin at Bubba Frey's store was, as we suspected, excellent – 'a commendable second place to Nook,' James wrote, 'but still not with the transcendent special taste.' Moving to Mowata was not on the table. Also, he and Susan and the Bonins' daughter Melissa had gone to dinner together and, as it happened, had fallen into a little chat about the future. 'I told her that if Emile learned the recipe and learned how to make boudin he'd never starve,' James said. 'And neither, it goes without saying, would we.'

First published in the *New Yorker*, 28 January 2002

Wonton Lust

My wife, Alice, doesn't want to go to Chinatown for Thanksgiving this year. 'Alice has changed,' I told friends when I learned of her decision. 'She's not the Alice we once knew.' But, then again, maybe she is. Now that I look back on those Thanksgiving meals – Alice and I and our two daughters in a Chinese restaurant, stuffing down some particularly festive fare, like minced squab in lettuce leaves – maybe she was the one member of the family who was lacking genuine enthusiasm.

I should explain that we are floaters on Thanksgiving. Alice has always been interested in a big Christmas celebration. (I've always felt the same way about Halloween; you might say it's a mixed marriage.) Given the proportions of the dinner we put on at Christmas every year, our holding a Thanksgiving dinner at home would be the equivalent of the Allies' deciding to invade some other continent five weeks before the Normandy landings, just to keep in practice.

I think a lot of people feel that Christmas and Thanksgiving are too close together to be celebrated by similar blowouts. Canadians, who have an international reputation for good sense, give thanks in October, which puts a little distance between the times you have to haul the extra chairs up from the basement and brace yourself for your Uncle Norton's dissertation on miles-per-gallon in autumn driving conditions. It may be significant that except in Toronto and Vancouver the Chinese-restaurant options in Canada tend to be rather grim.

In the early eighties, we had Thanksgiving at home for a couple of years. At the time, I was launching my campaign to change the national Thanksgiving dish from turkey to spaghetti carbonara – which I believe the Indians, having had some experience with Pilgrim cuisine, must have brought with them to the first Thanksgiving – and I thought we should set an example. Now that I think of it, Alice was never completely in the Spaghetti Carbonara Day spirit.

Once we began floating again, we were not over-burdened with invitations. In Alice's view, a hostess who knew she was going to be berated for having no sense of history simply because she was serving turkey instead of spaghetti carbonara might decide that, all in all, she'd rather listen to her Uncle Norton.

Even when a friend did phone to invite us for Thanksgiving, though, I would often say, 'Thanks, but we've got plans: we're going to Chinatown.' To me, it seemed logical. The Thanksgiving ritual is based on eating, and, in that spirit, what I particularly wanted to give thanks for was the Immigration Act of 1965. Until then, this country virtually excluded Chinese while letting in as many English people as cared to come – a policy that in culinary terms bordered on the suicidal. After 1965, it became increasingly safe in America to go out to dinner without carting along your own spaghetti carbonara.

Naturally, I'd speak during the meal about what Americans should be grateful for. 'If the Pilgrims had been followed to the New World only by other Pilgrims,' I'd say to the girls between bites of duck with Chinese flowering chives, 'we would now be eating overcooked cauliflower and warm gray meat. So count your blessings, ladies.'

Our daughters are grown now, but with both of them expected for Thanksgiving this year I took it for granted that we'd be eating in Chinatown. So did they. Among the Thanksgiving customs they said they were looking forward to were salt-and-pepper shrimp and lo mein with ginger and scallion. Then I heard Alice on the telephone with a friend of ours I'll call Nora, at whose house we'd celebrated a couple of Thanksgivings. Nora does a turkey-and-stuffing dinner that would make Norman Rockwell sorry he hadn't brought along his brushes and canvas. Alice was saying that we'd absolutely love to come for Thanksgiving this year.

I suppose I should have been able to foresee this turn of events several years ago, when Alice insisted one Thanksgiving that in addition to dinner in Chinatown we all go to a Broadway musical together, 'so there's something celebratory'. What could be more celebratory than minced squab in lettuce leaves? And what exactly does Thanksgiving have to do with Rodgers and Hart, who would have been put in the stocks by the Pilgrims for having a sense of melody?

'I just love going to Nora's for Thanksgiving,' she said

to me after she hung up the phone. 'And so do the girls. And so do you. You know you do.'

'I wonder if Nora would be willing to augment the cranberry sauce with a little take-out stuffed bean curd,' I said. 'Just for the sake of tradition.'

First published in the *New Yorker*, 1996

The Magic Bagel

My wife and I came up with differing interpretations of a conversation I had with our older daughter, Abigail, not long ago after a dim-sum lunch in Chinatown. Abigail, who lives in San Francisco, was in New York to present a paper at a conference. As a group of us trooped back toward Greenwich Village, where she'd grown up and where my wife, Alice, and I still live, Abigail and I happened to be walking together. 'Let's get this straight, Abigail,' I said, after we'd finished off some topic and had gone along in silence for a few moments. 'If I can find those gnarly little dark pumpernickel bagels that we used to get at Tanenbaum's, you'll move back to New York. Right?'

'Absolutely,' Abigail said.

When I reported that exchange to Alice, she said that Abigail was speaking ironically. I found it difficult to believe that anybody could be ironic about those bagels. They were almost black. Misshapen. Oniony. Abigail adored them. Both of my daughters have always taken bagels seriously. My younger daughter, Sarah, also lives in California – she's in Los Angeles – and she often complains about the bagels there being below her standards. For a while, I brought along a dozen bagels for Sarah whenever I went to L.A., but I finally decided that this policy was counterproductive. 'If a person prefers to live in California, which happens to be thousands of miles from her very own parents,' I told her, 'it seems to me appropriate that such a person eat California bagels. I understand that in some places out there if you buy a dozen wheat-germ bagels you get one bee-pollen bagel free.'

Abigail, it should be noted, always had bagel stand-ards at least as high as Sarah's. I have previously documented the moment when I realized that she was actually a New Yorker (until she was four or five, I had somehow thought of her as being from the same place I'm from, Kansas City): we were back in Missouri visiting my family, and she said, 'Daddy, how come in Kansas City the bagels taste like just round bread?' In other words, she knew the difference between those bagel-shaped objects available in American supermarkets and the authentic New York item that had been hand-rolled and boiled in a vat and then carefully baked by a member in good standing of the Bakery and Confectionery Work-ers International Union. My sadness at the evidence that she wasn't actually from my home town was offset by my pride in the evidence that she was precocious.

Would Proust have been ironic about the madeleine, particularly if he had fetched up in a place where you couldn't get a decent madeleine if your life depended on it? When my daughters were children, bagels were not only their staple food but also the food of important rituals. On Sunday mornings, I often took them to Hous-ton Street, on the Lower East Side. At Russ & Daughters, which is what New Yorkers call an appetizing store, we would buy Nova Scotia salmon – a transaction that took some time, since the daughters (of Joel Russ, the founder, who stared down at us from a splendid portrait on the wall) had to quit slicing fish now and then to tell me in glorious detail how adorable my girls were. Then we'd go next door to Ben's Dairy to get cream cheese and a delicacy known as baked farmer's cheese with scallions. Then we were at Tanenbaum's, a bakery that was probably best known for a large, dark loaf often referred to as Russian health bread. We were not there for Russian health bread.

'So you think she's just humoring her old dad?' I asked Alice, when we discussed the conversation I'd had with Abigail on the way back from Chinatown.

'I do.'

Alice was probably right. I understood that. Abigail enjoys living in California, and she's got a job there that she loves. Children grow up and lead lives of their own. Parents are supposed to accept that. Still, I decided that I'd look around for those pumpernickel bagels. As my father used to say, 'What could it hurt?'

* * *

It wasn't my first try. When the pumpernickel bagels disappeared, I immediately made serious inquiries. Without wanting to cast blame, I have to say that the disappearance occurred on Mutke's watch. Mutke's formal name is Hyman Perlmutter. In the early seventies, he bought Tanenbaum's Bakery and transformed it into the downtown branch of a bakery he ran eight or ten blocks away called Moishe's. For some time, Mutke carried Tanenbaum's full inventory. Then one day – I don't remember precisely when, but Abigail and Sarah were still living at home – the pumpernickel bagels were no longer there. Confronted with the facts, Mutke was sanguine. Those particular bagels weren't available anymore, he explained, but, as a special order, he could always provide me with a dozen or two just like them. Eventually, he did. I pulled one out of the bag. It was a smooth bagel, uniformly round. It was the color of cappuccino, heavy on the milk. It was a stranger to onions. It was not by any means Abigail's bagel.

I realize now, of course, that I gave up too easily. Sure, I stopped by to try the pumpernickel anytime I heard of a promising new bagel bakery – even if it was uptown, a part of the city I don't venture to unnecessarily. But I didn't make a systematic search. How was I to know that bagels can be instrumental in keeping families intact? This time, I was going to be thorough. I had read in Molly O'Neill's *New York Cook Book* about a place in Queens where bagels were made in the old-fashioned way. I figured that there must be similar places in Brooklyn neighborhoods with a large population of Orthodox Jews – Williamsburg, maybe, or Borough Park. I was prepared to go to the outer boroughs. But I thought it made sense to start back on Houston Street.

The area where Abigail and Sarah and I used to make our Sunday rounds has seen some changes over the years. The old tenement streets used to seem grim. Now they sport patches of raffish chic. On Orchard Street, around the corner from our Sunday-morning purveyors, stores that have traditionally offered bargains on fabrics and women's clothing and leather goods are punctuated by the sort of clothing store that has a rack of design magazines and a coffee bar and such a spare display of garments that you might think you're in the studio apartment of someone who has bizarre taste in cocktail dresses and no closet to keep them in. These days, the Lower East Side is a late-night destination – both Orchard and Ludlow have bars too hip to require a sign – and a cool place to live. After spending years listening to customers tell him that he ought to move Russ & Daughters uptown, Mark Federman, the son of one of the daughters, is renovating the apartments above the store and expressing gratitude that his grandfather held on to the building.

Ben's Dairy has closed, and Moishe's Bakery has moved to a tiny place around the corner. But Russ & Daughters has been carefully preserved to look pretty much the way it did when the founder himself still had his arms deep in the herring barrel. I figured Mark might have some information I could use, and he was bound to be sympathetic to the project: his daughter, Niki, recently graduated from college and moved to San Francisco. 'Do you think Niki might come back, too, if we found the bagels?' I asked, as Mark and I edged ourselves into the tiny office he shares with his wife, Maria.

'I don't think she'd come back for bagels,' he said. 'Maybe for an apartment upstairs.'

Maria shook her head. 'I already offered,' she said.

Mark said that he knew precisely the bagel I was talking about, but that he had no idea where to find it. He phoned his mother, who's retired, in Florida. 'Do you remember when Tanenbaum next door used to have this sort of gnarly – ' he began, and then started to laugh.

'Not an old woman,' he said. 'I'm asking about bagels.' Apparently, his mother remembered the gnarly old woman quite well. Not the bagels.

Although Russ & Daughters carries bagels these days, Mark insisted that he didn't have the expertise to be much help in tracing a particular baker; locating an obscure source of belly lox would have been more his line of country. Still, he made a couple of calls, including one to Mosha's Bread, a wholesale operation in Williamsburg, which has been turning out pumpernickel since the late nineteenth century. (Mosha's Bread, it almost goes without saying, has no connection with Moishe's Bakery.) As I was about to leave Russ's, the boss of Mosha's, who turned out to be a woman named Cecile Erde Farkas, returned Mark's call. Mark introduced himself, and before he could explain my quest he began to sound like someone on the receiving end of a sales pitch. 'To tell you the truth, I don't sell much bread,' I heard him say, and then, 'Here's what I could use – a good babka. I could sell the hell out of a good babka . . . plain, yeah, and chocolate.'

* * *

There was a message on my answering machine that evening from Mark. He had reached a friend of his named Danny Scheinin, who ran Kossar's, a distinguished purveyor of bialys, for decades before selling out a year or two ago. 'Danny says he thinks Tanenbaum got that bagel from somebody named Poznanski,' Mark said, when I got back to him. 'Also, he says it wasn't a real bagel.'

'Not a real bagel!'

'I don't know exactly what he means,' Mark said. 'Talk to him.'

When I reached Scheinin, I found out that what he'd meant was this: In the old days, there was a sharp split between bagel bakeries and bread bakeries. The bagel bakers had their own local, No. 338. They didn't bake bread and bread bakers didn't make bagels. Originally, of course, bagels were made only with white flour. But some bread bakers who trafficked in pumpernickel would twist some bread dough into bagel shapes and bake them. By not going through the intermediate boiling that is part of the process of making an authentic bagel, they stayed out of another local's jurisdiction. Scheinin was confident that Abigail's bagel had been made that way for Tanenbaum's by a bread baker named Sam Poznanski, in Williamsburg, who died some years ago. As far as Scheinin knew, the bakery still existed, under the management of Poznanski's wife. He gave me the number. 'Tell her Danny from the bialys said to call,' he told me.

Mrs. Poznanski, I have to say, did not seem terribly engaged by my quest. The longest answer she gave was when I asked her if Poznanski's had quit making the pumpernickel bagel when her husband died, and she said, 'No. Before.' Still, she confirmed that the object of Abigail's adoration was from Poznanski's and that it was not boiled. This was hard news to take. It sounded perilously close to saying that the bagel we were searching for was just round bread. But what bread!

The bread/bagel split was confirmed by Herb Bostick, a business agent of Local 3 of the Bakery and Confectionery Workers International Union, which by now has absorbed No. 338 into a local that mixes bagel bakers and bread bakers and cake bakers together the way someone faced with baking a pie at the last minute might mix in bits of whatever kinds of flour happened to be in the cupboard. What Bostick said was in line with what I'd learned from Cecile Farkas, of Mosha's, with whom I'd arranged a meeting after her babka pitch to Mark. She'd told me that for years her late father offered pumpernickel bagels that were baked without being boiled first. 'Then they weren't real bagels?' I'd said.

'If my daddy called them bagels they were bagels,' Mrs. Farkas said.

I hadn't had to journey to the outer boroughs to see Cecile Farkas. By chance, she was doing a bread promotion at a store on Twenty-third Street. She turned out to be a chatty woman in her sixties, who told me that she had joined Mosha's only when her father became elderly; she'd been trained as an electrical engineer. That didn't surprise me. Mark Federman had been a lawyer. A family business is no respecter of degrees. Mrs. Farkas told me that her own daughter, having earned her master's in career counselling, plans to launch Mosha's West. Would Mosha's West be a few blocks closer to Manhattan than the original Mosha's? No. Her daughter lives in San Francisco. Cecile Farkas said that, with only a few hours' notice, Mosha's could duplicate the sort of bagel Abigail craves. 'It would be my pleasure,' she said.

'If that happens and Abigail moves back to New York, you would have done a mitzvah,' I said. 'It would be written next to your name in the Book of Life.'

Mrs. Farkas shrugged off any thought of reward. 'It

would be my pleasure,' she repeated. I had recognized her as a person of character the moment she'd told me that whatever her daddy said was a bagel was a bagel.

* * *

I tried to present the situation to Alice in an objective way: 'I suppose you think that if Mosha's really did succeed in duplicating the bagel and I told Abigail that it was readily available in the neighborhood and I didn't trouble her with the really quite arcane information that it's not, technically speaking, a bagel, I would be acting completely contrary to everything we tried to teach her about honesty and integrity.'

'Yes,' Alice said.

'I thought you might.'

She's right, of course. I know that. Lately, though, it has occurred to me that there were areas I left unexplored in my conversation with Mrs. Poznanski. It's true that she expressed no interest whatsoever in bagels, but what if I got Mark Federman to agree to carry those little pumpernickel numbers – not instead of Mrs. Farkas's babkas, I hasten to say, but in addition to Mrs. Farkas's babkas. Would the Russ & Daughters account be enough to propel Poznanski's back into the bagel business? This is assuming, of course, that Sam Poznanski's recipe still exists. All in all, it's a long shot. Still, I'm thinking of making a trip to Williamsburg. What could it hurt?

First published in the *New Yorker*, 27 March 2000

Killer Bagels

I was surprised to read that bagels have become the most dangerous food in the country. I've lived in New York – which is to bagels what Paris is to croissants – for a number of years, and I've never been injured by a bagel. When I go back to Kansas City, where I grew up, old friends never say, 'Isn't it scary living in New York, what with the bagels and all?' My answer to that question would be that New Yorkers who were asked to name foods they think of as particularly benign would mention bagels as often as chicken soup.

They might talk about that morning in the park when nothing seemed to soothe their crying baby until a grandmotherly woman sitting on a nearby bench, nattering with another senior citizen about Social Security payments or angel-food-cake recipes or Trotskyism, said that the only thing for a teething infant was a day-old bagel. They might talk about the joy of returning to New York from a long sojourn in a place that was completely without bagels – Bangladesh, or a tiny town in Montana, or some other outpost in the vast patches of the world that New Yorkers tend to think of as the Bagel Barrens. They might talk about the days when people used to sit on their stoops and watch the neighborhood kids play roller-skate hockey in the street with a stale bagel as the puck – days spent listening contentedly to the comforting slap of hockey stick against bagel and the inevitable cries, when the action got too close to a drain opening, 'Lost bagel! Lost bagel!' They might talk about picking up freshly baked bagels late at night and being reassured, as they felt the warmth coming through the brown paper bag, that they would be at peace with the world the next morning, at least through breakfast.

According to a piece in the *Times* not long ago about how dangerous kitchens have become, that brown paper bag could have been holding a time bomb. 'We're seeing an increasing number of bagel-related injuries in the emergency service,' Dr. Stephen Adams, associate medical director of the emergency department at Northwestern Memorial Hospital, in Chicago, told the author of the piece, Suzanne Hamlin. It isn't that bagels are considered dangerous to eat in the way that triple bacon cheeseburgers are considered dangerous to eat. It's true that in recent years some bakers in New York have been making bagels with some pretty weird ingredients – oat bran, say, and cinnamon, and more air than you'd find in the Speaker of the House – but not dangerously weird. Nor is there any implication that bagels are dangerous because they are easily flung at people in the close quarters of an apartment kitchen.

The danger comes with people trying to get at bagels. 'The hand lacerations, cuts, gouges and severed digits,' it says in the *Times*, 'are caused by impatient eaters who try to pry apart frozen bagels with screwdrivers, attempt to cut hard bagels with dull knives and, more than likely, use their palms as cutting boards.'

Ms. Hamlin found no increase in New York bagel

injuries. Reading about the havoc that bagels can wreak in Illinois or California, a New Yorker might say, in the superior tone customarily used by someone from Minneapolis describing the chaos caused in Birmingham by a simple snowstorm, 'People there just don't know how to handle such things' – or, as the director of emergency medicine at Bellevue said to the *Times*, 'Those people just aren't ethnically equipped.' The Bagel Barrens have been shrinking rapidly – bagel stores have sprouted in the shopping malls of neighborhoods that baked-goods sociologists have long identified with white bread – so maybe it's true that a lot of Americans are being given access to bagels before they know how to handle them, in the way that a lot of Americans are said to have access to 9-mm. pistols or semiautomatic rifles before they know how to handle them.

But there is a more positive way to look at this. Twenty years ago, the bagels in Kansas City were accurately described by one of my daughters as tasting like 'round bread'. It was impossible to conceive of anybody desperately going to work with a screwdriver to free up one of them for thawing. Could it be that outlander bagels have improved to the point of being something that people truly yearn for? If so, maybe what we're seeing in Midwestern emergency rooms is the price of progress.

First published in the *New Yorker*, 1996

Don't Mention It

I suppose Kenny Shopsin, who runs a small restaurant a couple of blocks from where I live in Greenwich Village, could qualify as eccentric in a number of ways, but one of his views seems particularly strange to journalists who have had prolonged contact with proprietors of retail businesses in New York: he hates publicity. I've tried not to take this personally. I have been a regular customer, mainly at lunch, since 1982, when Kenny and his wife, Eve, turned a corner grocery store they had been running on the same premises into a thirty-four-seat café. Before that, I was a regular customer of the grocery store. When the transformation was made, my daughters were around junior-high-school age, and even now, grown and living out of the city, they consider Shopsin's General Store – or Ken and Eve's or Kenny's, as they usually call it – an extension of their kitchen. Normally, they take only a brief glance at the menu – a menu that must include about nine hundred items, some of them as unusual as Cotton Picker Gumbo Melt Soup or Hanoi Hoppin John with Shrimp or Bombay Turkey Cloud Sandwich – and then order dishes that are not listed, such as 'tomato soup the way Sarah likes it' or 'Abigail's chow fun'.

When Kenny gets a phone call from a restaurant guidebook that wants to include Shopsin's, he sometimes says that the place is no longer in operation, identifying himself as someone who just happens to be there moving out the fixtures. Some years ago, a persistent English guidebook carried a generally complimentary review of Shopsin's that started with a phrase like 'Although it has no décor'. Eve expressed outrage, not simply at the existence of the review but also at its content. 'Do you call this "no décor"?' she demanded of me one evening when I was there having an early supper – the only kind of supper you can have at Shopsin's, which has not strayed far from grocery-store hours. (Aside from a Sunday brunch that began as a sort of family project several months ago, the restaurant has never been open on weekends.) She waved her arm to take in the entire establishment.

I looked around. Shopsin's still looks a lot like a corner store. It has an old pressed-tin ceiling. There are shelves, left over from the grocery store, that are always piled high and not terribly neatly with ingredients and supplies. There are always newspapers and magazines around for the customer who might need reading material while eating alone. A table setup might include a constantly varying assortment of toys and puzzles – a custom that started when the Shopsins' children were young and continues for the more or less grownup customers. The counter, which no longer has stools, is taken up mainly by buckets of complimentary penny candy. One wall has, in addition to a three-dimensional advertisement for Oscar Mayer beef franks, some paintings of the place and its denizens. The portrait of Kenny shows him as a bushy-haired man with a baby face that makes him look younger than he is, which is nearly sixty, and a girth that may reflect years of tasting his more remarkable creations; he's wearing a Shopsin's General Store T-shirt, folded over in the way the cognoscenti know how to fold it in order to form the words 'Eat Me'. A large sign behind the tiny kitchen that Kenny shares with his longtime assistant, José, says 'All Our Cooks Wear Condoms'. When I had taken in all of that, or whatever part of it was there at the time, I said, 'I absolutely agree, Eve. A reviewer might comment on whether or not the décor is to his taste. Conceivably, he could prefer another type of décor. But you can't say that this place has no décor.'

Normally, mentions of Shopsin's in print are complimentary, in a sort of left-handed way – as in *Time Out New York's* most recent guide to the city's restaurants, which raved about the soups and described Kenny ('the foul-mouthed middle-aged chef and owner') as 'a culinary genius, if for no other reason than he figured out how to fit all his ingredients into such a tiny restaurant'. To Kenny's way of thinking, a complimentary mention is worse than a knock. It brings review-trotters – the sort of people who go to a restaurant because somebody told them to. Kenny finds that review-trotters are often 'petulant and demanding'. Failing to understand that they are not in a completely conventional restaurant, they may be taken aback at having the person next to them contribute a sentence or two to their conversation or at hearing Kenny make a general remark in language not customarily heard in company unless the company is in a locker room or at being faced with deciding among nine hundred items and then, if they have selected certain dishes, having to indicate the degree of spiciness on a scale of one to ten. (Before Shopsin's began restricting its serving staff to Eve, it employed a waitress who narrowed at least that choice by refusing to take an order higher than a six, on humanitarian grounds.)

Ken and Eve have found that review-trotters often don't know their own minds. If a customer at Shopsin's seems completely incapable of deciding what to order, Eve will, in the interest of saving time, reveal her own favorites, which these days happen to be three dishes with chicken in them – Chicken Tortilla Avocado Soup, Pecan Chicken Wild Rice Cream Enchilada, and Taco Fried Chicken. But she doesn't do it with a song in her heart. Kenny is less flexible. 'If somebody comes in here and is flabbergasted by the number of things on the menu and tells me, "How can I choose?"' he has said, 'I realize that they're essentially in the wrong restaurant.'

The place can handle just so many people, and Kenny was never interested in an expansion that would transform him into a supervisor. 'The economic rhythm of this place is that I run fifteen meals a week,' he used to say before Shopsin's offered Sunday brunch. 'If I do any five of them big, I break even; if I do ten of them big, I'll make money. I'll make a lot of money. But if I do fifteen I have to close, because it's too much work.' Kenny requires slow periods for recouping energy and ingredients. The techniques that enable him to offer as many dishes as he does are based on the number of people he has to serve rather than on what they order. That's why he won't do takeout, and that's one of the reasons parties of five are told firmly that the restaurant does not serve groups larger than four. Pretending to be a party of three that happened to have come in with a party of two is a very bad idea.

Not all the rules at Shopsin's are based on the number of meals that the kitchen has to put out. For years, a rule against copying your neighbor's order was observed fairly strictly. Customers who had just arrived might ask someone at the next table the name of the scrumptious-looking dish he was eating. Having learned that it was Burmese Hummus – one of my favorites, as it happens, even though it is not hummus and would not cause pangs of nostalgia in the most homesick Burmese – they might order Burmese Hummus, only to have Eve shake her head wearily. No copying. That rule eventually got downgraded into what Ken called 'a strong tradition', and has now pretty much gone by the wayside. 'I realized that the problem was not that they were trying to imitate the other person but that they weren't capable of ordering anything themselves, and it was just unnecessary cruelty to point that out to them,' Kenny told me not long ago. He said he was getting more and more people of that sort.

'Why is that?' I asked.

'The country's going that way,' he said glumly.

Because Shopsin's has a number of rules and because Kenny is, by his own admission, 'not a patient person', it's common to run into people who are afraid to enter the place. I've escorted a number of them to their first Shopsin's meal, in the way a longtime businessman in a Midwestern town might escort a newcomer to Kiwanis at noon on Wednesday. Since the 'Seinfeld' Soup Nazi episode became part of the culture, people sometimes compare Kenny to the brilliant but rule-obsessed soup purveyor who terrified Jerry Seinfeld and his friends. Kenny would say that one difference between him and the Soup Nazi is that the Soup Nazi is shown ladling out his soup from a steam table; at Shopsin's, most soups are made from scratch when they're ordered.

Some people think of Shopsin's as forbiddingly clubby, chilly to outsiders. Actually, Shopsin's does not have a crowd, in the sense of a group of people who go in assuming they'll run into someone they know – the way the old Lion's Head, a few blocks uptown, had a crowd, built around *Village Voice* writers. At a play reading once, I was surprised to run into a Shopsin's regular I hadn't realized was an actor; all I'd known about him was that he doted on a dish called Turkey Spinach Cashew Brown Rice Burrito. Still, there are a lot of regulars, and they seem more at home than they might at a conventional restaurant. 'You're really not allowed to be anonymous here,' Kenny has said. 'You have to be willing to be who you really are. And that scares a lot of people.' One evening, when the place was nearly full, I saw a party of four come in the door; a couple of them may have been wearing neckties, which wouldn't have been a plus in a restaurant whose waitress used to wear a T-shirt that said 'Die Yuppie Scum.' Kenny took a quick glance from the kitchen and said, 'No, we're closed.' After a brief try at appealing the decision, the party left, and the waitress pulled the security gate partway down to discourage other latecomers.

'It's only eight o'clock,' I said to Kenny.

'They were nothing but strangers,' he said.

'I think those are usually called customers,' I said. 'They come here, you give them food, they give you money. It's known as the restaurant business.'

Kenny shrugged. 'Fuck 'em,' he said.

*   *   *

Anytime there seemed to be a threat of my becoming entangled in a piece of unauthorized publicity about Shopsin's, I have resorted to rank cowardice, spooked by the fear of a lifetime banishment that might not even carry the possibility of parole. Once, I asked Kenny if an acquaintance of mine who'd been eighty-sixed some years before but greatly missed the place and its proprietors could come in for lunch with me sometime. 'Sure, she can come in for lunch,' Kenny said. 'And I'll tell her she's a scumbag bitch.' I told him I might hold off on that lunch for a while.

In the mid-nineties, I got a phone call from a reporter named D. T. Max, who was doing a piece for the New York *Observer* on Shopsin's, without the cooperation of the proprietor. After assuring him of my belief that reporters have an obligation to talk to other reporters on the record and informing him that I had been quoted by name insulting most of the people I've ever worked for, I told him that in this instance I intended to be exceedingly circumspect and to keep Kenny informed of everything I said. Max was most understanding.

When I did report back to Kenny, I was asked what information I had surrendered. 'Well, the subject of

Egyptian Burritos came up,' I said. Egyptian Burrito was then listed on the breakfast menu, although I'd never eaten one. On the rare occasions that I had been to Shopsin's for what people in some other trades might call a breakfast meeting, I'd always allocated my calories to Shred Potatoes, a fabulous dish that Kenny claims to have stolen from a short-order cook in the Carolinas through intense observation that required only ten minutes.

'And?' Kenny asked.

'Well, he seemed interested in what an Egyptian Burrito was,' I said.

'So what did you say?'

'I said, "An Egyptian Burrito is a burrito, and inside is sort of what Kenny thinks Egyptians might eat."'

Kenny considered that for a moment. 'Well, that's accurate,' he finally said. He sounded relieved. By chance, though, the *Observer* piece ended with an anecdote, accurately gathered from someone else, that involved me: One morning, a Sanitation Department officer had come in to ticket Kenny for some minor infraction like wrapping his garbage incorrectly or putting it in the wrong place. Kenny, who was at the stove, lost his temper and threw a handful of flour he happened to be holding at the sanitation officer, who thereupon summoned a police officer to write a citation. When I was told about the incident at lunch that day, I asked Kenny, 'What was the citation for – assault with intent to bake?' A couple of months after Max's piece appeared, Kenny said he had finally concluded that I, frustrated at not having been able to work the assault-with-intent-to-bake line in anywhere, might have instigated an article in the

Observer just to get it into print. I had a defense for that: within days of my exchange with Kenny about flour-throwing, I had, without mentioning any names, eased the anecdote into a newspaper column that was on a completely different subject.

Yes, I've managed to write about Shopsin's from time to time, always observing the prohibition against mentioning its name or location. That is one reason I've never been offended by Kenny's refusal to recognize a reporter's God-given right to turn absolutely everything into copy. In a piece about Greenwich Village a few years ago, for instance, I asked a restaurant proprietor 'who tends not to be cordial to people wearing suits' what the difference was between the Village and uptown, and he said, 'I don't know. I've never been uptown.' Kenny has never objected to any of the mentions. He has always thought of us as being in similar fields, and, as someone who has to be prepared every day to turn out any one of nine hundred dishes a customer might ask for, he has a deep understanding of waste not, want not.

In the mid-seventies, in fact, when my daughters were little girls, I wrote an entire article for this magazine about a corner store in the West Village which was run with rare imagination and a warm feeling for community – a store with a rocking chair and bean-counting contests and free circulating paperback books. At that time, the store struck me as being about as close as Greenwich Village got to the Village conjured up by reading, say, 'My Sister Eileen' – even to the point of having a proprietor, described in the piece as a young man from a prosperous background who'd always had what he called 'a little trouble with authority', capable of making occasional allusions to Camus or Sartre as he sliced the roast beef. At the time, Kenny owned some dazzling old gumball machines, and I simply referred to Shopsin's by the name my girls always used – the Bubble Gum Store.

So why am I calling it Shopsin's now? Because not long ago Kenny told me that it was no longer necessary to abide by the rule against mentioning the place in print. The building that Shopsin's is in, an undistinguished five-story brick structure that consists of the restaurant and eight apartments, changed hands several months ago. Kenny, who was faced with having to re-negotiate his lease, at first treated the situation philosophically. When I asked him what the new owner, Robert A. Cohen, of R. A. Cohen & Associates, was like, he shrugged and said, 'He's a real-estate guy,' in the tone that New Yorkers customarily use to mean that asking for further details would be naïve. Then Kenny and Cohen had a meeting at Cohen's office. ('I went uptown!' Kenny told me, as a way of emphasizing a willingness to put himself out.) According to Kenny, Cohen offered the Shopsins a one-year lease at more or less market rent. He also offered a three-year lease, contingent on one of their daughters vacating a rent-stabilized apartment she occupies in the building. A one-year lease is obviously not practical for a restaurant, and the attempt to include Kenny's daughter in the transaction did not please him. All in all, I would say that Robert A. Cohen was fortunate that the offers were made when Kenny wasn't holding a handful of flour.

Kenny decided that he would leave at the end of May rather than sign a new lease. He hopes to reopen nearby. He is aware, though, that the tone of his business has a lot to do with the physical space it has occupied for more than thirty years, including what I suppose you'd have to call the décor – the old-fashioned booths that Kenny ran across and cut down to fit his space, the music from tapes he puts together himself from songs of the twenties and thirties (supplanted, occasionally, by a modern Finnish group that concentrates on the tango). Kenny says that what really distinguishes his place from other restaurants is the level of human involvement in every detail. As he has put it, 'I've been peeing on every hydrant around here for thirty years.' In other words, the Shopsin's my daughters have known – Kenny's, Ken and Eve's, the Bubble Gum Store – can no longer be affected by publicity because it will no longer exist.

* * *

The God of New York real estate is an ironic god, and he works in ironic ways. What propelled Ken and Eve into the restaurant business in the first place, twenty years ago, was a bump in their rent. They figured that their choices were to start opening on weekends or transform the store into a restaurant. By that time, Kenny was doing a good business in takeout sandwiches like chicken salad and egg salad. 'Zito would bring me over bread and I would just have a line out the door every lunchtime,' he recalled not long ago. 'Essentially, if any-one asked me what I did for a living, I said I sold mayonnaise – mayonnaise with chicken, mayonnaise with shrimp, mayonnaise with eggs, mayonnaise with potatoes. The key was that essentially you sold mayonnaise for eight dollars a pound and everything else you threw in for free.' He had also been making what he calls 'restaurant-style food to take out of a non-restaurant' – turkey dinner every Wednesday, for instance, and chicken pot pie. When Ken and Eve closed the store for the summer – because they had young children, Shopsin's was the rare Village business that often observed the *fermeture annuelle* – Ken, a reasonably adept handyman who had worked as a building superintendent before he went into the grocery business, turned Shopsin's General Store into a restaurant. When it opened, the menu listed a conventional number of more or less conventional dishes, although there was some hint of the future in items like Yiddishe Melt (grilled American cheese on rye over grilled Jewish salami) and Linda's Frito Pie, a Texas specialty whose recipe has to begin, 'Take a bag of Fritos . . .'

Kenny had Frito Pie on the menu because one of his customers, who's from Texas, was comforted by the knowledge that less than a block from her house in Greenwich Village she could order a dish that most Texans identify with the snack bar at Friday-night high-school football games. The menu grew because of what customers wanted or what Kenny was struck by in reading cookbooks or what new ingredient he happened across or what he figured out how to do as he taught himself to cook. 'I don't make too many decisions,' Kenny once told me. 'I react.' Lately, for instance, a lot of dishes have been inspired by the tchotchkes he's bought on eBay. Because of some tortilla bowls he snapped up for a bargain price, he is now offering Mexican moo shu pork, which can also be ordered with chicken or turkey and has something in common with a former dish called Thai Turkey Torpedo. Some large plastic bowls split in two by a curving divider led to what he calls Yin/Yang Soups – a couple of dozen soups and a couple of dozen kinds of rice that can be ordered in any combination, like Sweet Potato Cream Curry Soup with Piña Colada Rice or Toasted Pumpkin Seed Soup with Ricotta Pignoli Rice.

There is almost no danger of a customer's ordering Plantain Pulled Turkey Soup with Strawberry BBQ Rice only to find out that there isn't any more Plantain Pulled Turkey Soup and he might have to settle for, say, Mashed Potato Radish Soup. In the twenty years my family has been eating at Shopsin's, putting our meals on the tab we established when Ken and Eve were selling milk and paper towels and cat food, nobody at our table has ever ordered anything the restaurant was out of. When I asked Eve recently if that held true with other customers, she said that she thinks she remembers running out of chicken cutlets sometime within the past year.

'I think I have everything all the time,' Kenny says. 'That's part of the system.' What does happen occasionally is that Kenny gets an idea for a dish and writes on the specials board – yes, there is a specials board – something like Indomalekian Sunrise Stew. (Kenny and his oldest son, Charlie, invented the country of Indomalekia along with its culinary traditions.) A couple of weeks later, someone finally orders Indomalekian Sunrise Stew and

Kenny can't remember what he had in mind when he thought it up. Fortunately, the customer doesn't know, either, so Kenny just invents it again on the spot.

* * *

As the menu at Shopsin's grew, I half expected to come in for lunch one day and find Kenny being peered at intently by a team of researchers from the institution that foodies are referring to when they mention the C.I.A. – the Culinary Institute of America – or maybe even a team from the other C.I.A. The researchers would have their work cut out for them. It's true that if you listen to Kenny talk about cooking for a while, you can see the outline of some general strategies. For instance, he freezes pre-portioned packages of some ingredients that take a long time to cook and then pops them into the microwave – 'nuking 'em' for a couple of minutes – while he's doing the dish. He fiddles with his equipment, so that he's drilled out the holes on one burner of his stove and rigged up a sort of grid on another. He runs a new idea or a new ingredient through a large part of his menu. ('I love permutations.') On the other hand, Kenny has said, 'There's no unifying philosophy. I do a lot of things special, and not only do I do a lot of things special but I commingle them.'

To get an idea of Kenny's methods, I once asked him how he made one of Eve's favorites, Chicken Tortilla Avocado Soup, which he describes as a simple soup. 'When someone orders that, I put a pan up with oil in it,' he said. 'Not olive oil; I use, like, a Wesson oil. And I leave it. I've drilled out the holes in the burner so . . . it's really fucking hot . . . On the back burner, behind where that pan is, I have that grid. I just take a piece of chicken breast and throw it on. The grid is red hot, flames shooting up, and the chicken sears with black marks immediately and starts to cook. If there were grits or barley or something, I would nuke 'em . . . At that point in the cook, that's what would happen if this were Chicken Tortilla Avocado with barley in it. For this dish – this is a fast dish – I shred cabbage with my knife. Green cabbage . . . I cut off a chunk and I chop it really finely into long, thin shreds. I do the same with a piece of onion. Same with fresh cilantro. At this point, José has turned the chicken while my back is still to the pan. I throw the shit into the oil, and if you rhythm it properly, by the time you have the onions and everything cut, the oil is just below smoke. Smoke for that oil is about three-eighty-five. After three-eighty-five, you might as well throw it out. It won't fry anymore; it's dead. But I turn around just before smoke and I throw this shit in. And what happens is the cabbage hits it and almost deep-fries – it browns – and now we get a really nice cabbage, Russian-type flavor. The onions soften immediately, and I now turn back and I take one of any number of ingredients, depending on what they've ordered, and in this particular instance, for someone like you, I would add crushed-up marinated jalapeño peppers to about a five, which is about a half a tablespoon. They're in a little cup in front of me . . . In front of me, in, like, a desk in-out basket, I have two levels of vegetables that don't need to be refrigerated and I have plastic cups full of garlic or whatever. So now the soup is cooking. So then I reach under the refrigerator. On the refrigerator floor there's another thirty or forty ingredients, and I'll take for this particular soup hominy – canned yellow hominy – and throw in a handful of that. Then I go to the steam table and take from the vegetarian black-bean soup – it has a slotted spoon in it – a half spoon of vegetarian cooked black beans. And then I switch to the right, because the spice rack is there, and I put in a little cumin. Then I take the whole thing and I pour chicken stock in it from the steam table. And at this point José has already taken the chicken off the flame. The chicken now is marked on the outside and the outside is white, but it's not cooked. It's pink in the center. He cuts it into strips, we throw it into the soup, a cover goes on the soup, it gets moved over to the left side of the stove on a lower light and in about three minutes José takes a bowl, puts some tortilla chips that I've fried the day before in the bowl with some sliced avocado and then pours the soup over it. And that's Chicken Tortilla Avocado Soup.' There are about two hundred other soups.

Presumably, Kenny can arrange his ingredients around a customized stove in some other storefront. Presumably, it will be convenient to our house. The last time I discussed the move with him, he mentioned a couple of possibilities. One is convenient, but it's somewhat larger than the present restaurant and it seems less vulnerable to being shaped by Kenny's personality. Another has the appropriate funkiness but also has what everyone, Kenny included, believes is 'the world's worst location'. That tempts Kenny, of course. He is someone whose contrariness is so ingrained that he can begin a description of one cooking experiment like this: 'At the time I was interested in baba ghanouj, I was reading a James Beard article about eggplants and he said never put eggplants in a microwave. So I went and put an eggplant in a microwave . . .'

When Kenny mentioned that the second place was on such an awful block that my daughters and I would probably come only once, I assured him of their loyalty, assuming he continued to turn out 'tomato soup the way Sarah likes it' and 'Abigail's chow fun'. They confirmed this when I phoned them to bring them up to date on the latest Shopsin's developments. They also expressed some concern about the possibility that writing about Shopsin's even now carried the risk of causing overcrowding or inadvertently saying something that could lead to the banishment of the author – and, presumably, his progeny.

'Don't worry,' I told one of them. 'Kenny says it's O.K.'

'Just be careful,' she said.

First published in the *New Yorker*, 15 April 2002

Where's Chang?

When I think about who might be the most devoted and influential Changian I've met – the closest equivalent to what the food Web site chowhound.com used to call its Alpha Dog – the person who usually comes to mind is John Binkley, a retired Washington economist who now lives in Franklin, North Carolina. I hasten to say that, as far as I know, Binkley has never used the word 'Changian' to describe himself, although I suspect that he would prefer it to 'groupie', which he has occasionally been called, or 'obsessive', which he has acknowledged being, or 'somewhat like the people who used to follow the Grateful Dead', which is how he was once described on DonRockwell.com, a Washington food Web site visited regularly by Binkley and those similarly afflicted. Binkley is a follower of a mysteriously peripatetic Chinese chef named Peter Chang – follower not only in the sense of being a devotee but also in the sense of having literally followed Chang from restaurant to restaurant, as soon as it became clear where, in the Southeastern quadrant of the United States, that restaurant happened to be.

Among contributors to food blogs and forums, it is common to dream of wandering into some dreary-looking chowmein joint called Bamboo Gardens or Golden Dragon, ordering a couple of items you hadn't expected to see on the menu, and discovering that the kitchen harbors a chef of spectacular ability. In 2005, Binkley and some other serious eaters began patronizing a modestly priced strip-mall restaurant in Fairfax, Virginia, called China Star, which, in addition to providing the usual Americanized Chinese staples, seemed capable of producing some remarkable Szechuanese cuisine. They eventually learned that China Star's chef was Peter Chang, who had won national cooking competitions in China and had served as chef at the Chinese Embassy. It occurred to some of them that they had found the chef of their dreams. The only problem was that, like a lot of the people who inhabit dreams, he had a tendency to disappear.

Binkley is hardly the only candidate for Alpha Dog of the Changian movement. Writing in the Washington *City Paper* later that year, Todd Kliman raved about the food being produced by Chang, who by then had left China Star and had been found again in an Alexandria restaurant whose name, TemptAsian, made it sound like a Japanese phone-sex operation. In May of 2006, after Kliman had switched to *Washingtonian*, he wrote a rapturous review of Chang's food at yet another place of business – Szechuan Boy, in Fairfax. Kliman reported that at Szechuan Boy Chang was better than ever at some of his signature dishes – Roast Fish with Green Onions, for instance, which was described as 'really, a heaping plate of expertly fried fish, dusted with cumin, topped off with chopped ginger, fried parsley and diced chilies and served in a thatched bamboo pouch'. Kliman, who has eaten in every one of Chang's restaurants, remains devoted to the master ('I think I'd rather eat his food than anyone's'), but you could argue that, as a professional restaurant critic, he has just been doing his duty, however much he may have enjoyed it.

Kliman believes that the Chang frenzy has been driven by the Internet rather than by reviews – by people who savor the thrill of deconstructing complicated dishes and correcting each other on arcane points of culinary authenticity or grammar. It has never been unusual, of course, for a restless chef of prodigious talent to be pursued by loyal fans. Years ago, in my own home town of Kansas City, the fried-chicken fancy passed around information on the whereabouts of a gifted pan-fryer known as Chicken Betty Lucas the way they might selectively disclose a particularly valuable stock tip. (Toward the end of Chicken Betty's wanderings – she was then cooking at the coffee shop of the Metro Auto Auction, in Lee's Summit – I asked her why she had moved around so much, and she said, 'Life's too short to work where you're unhappy.') But the Internet has made such pursuits more efficient and more intense, and more, well, obsessive.

James Glucksman, another important figure in the Changian movement, has been a steady user of the Internet, sometimes under the nom de blog Pandahugga. Having mastered Mandarin after switching from Russian Studies to Chinese Studies at Columbia (partly, he says, because of the food), Glucksman may have been the first Changian to speak directly to Chang in a language the chef understood. An early patron of China Star, Glucksman helped Chang translate the menu for TemptAsian. His linguistic skills and his experience with Chinese food are said to have been central to the efforts of a band of Changians who, during the summer of 2005, met at TemptAsian weekly in an effort to eat their way through the menu. But then Glucksman took a job in Beijing, and for several years now he has had to make do with the cooking of Chinese chefs in China. It was John Binkley who, through posts on food forums, gathered the troops for the attempt to consume everything TemptAsian offered. They failed to reach their goal in a way that I suspect most of them found satisfying: according to one of those present, Ken Flower, who works with computers for the federal government between meals, progress was slow because 'there were too many dishes we couldn't bear not to repeat.'

I heard about Peter Chang from another participant in the weekly assault on the TemptAsian menu – Stephen Banker, a Washington journalist I'd met during the time he was doing interviews for the Canadian Broadcasting Corporation. As I recall, Stephen e-mailed me during one of the periods when Chang's followers had completely lost his trail. Szechuan Boy had turned out to be his briefest stop. Apparently, many readers of Kliman's review rushed right over – although some of them must have turned back in confusion, since the sign above the entrance of Szechuan Boy still identified it as the restaurant it had replaced, China Gourmet. Soon, reports began filtering in about huge crowds but so-so food. 'The guy who bought that restaurant bought it on the premise that he was going to get Chef Chang to come with him and make it a real destination Chinese restaurant,' James Glucksman later told me. 'And that worked out fine for about two months. But then it got discovered, and they could not cope with the number of people who were coming.' Before the Szechuan Boy sign arrived, Chang was gone. No one knew where he was. One rumor on the Internet had it that he was still somewhere nearby. According to other rumors, he may have gone to Georgia or maybe Ohio.

It took John Binkley nearly six months to find him. In September of 2006, Binkley, who had recently moved from Washington to Franklin, was browsing the Southern boards of Chowhound when his eye fell on a post by Steve Drucker, an enthusiastic eater in Atlanta. Drucker mentioned hearing from the proprietor of a local Chinese restaurant that a prize-winning chef had come to the area. What's this! Binkley thought. Franklin, which is at the western end of North Carolina, is only about two and a half hours from Atlanta, and Binkley has made the trip regularly, often to buy Asian ingredients for cooking at home. He arranged to meet Drucker at the restaurant Drucker had sniffed out from the tip – Tasty China, in Marietta, a nearby county seat that has been swallowed into metropolitan Atlanta.

When Binkley entered Tasty China, he glanced over at the wall for the display he had seen at other Chang restaurants – two framed cooking-competition certificates, draped with accompanying medals, and photographs of Chang with the dignitaries he has cooked for. There they were. A few minutes later, Peter Chang and John Binkley were hugging and slapping each other on the back. That day, refraining from any 'Chef Chang, I presume' theatrics, Binkley wrote on DonRockwell.com, 'I had lunch in his new place today, in the company of a knowledgeable Atlanta chow-head. We had a few of the old standby's and one off-the-menu item he did up special: crispy eggplant cut like French fries and salt-fried with scallion greens, a hint of cumin, and hot pepper. To die for!' Binkley's good fortune did not last long. In the spring of 2007, posts from people who suspected that Chang was no longer in the kitchen of Tasty China began showing up on chowhound.com. Finally, in an April post, Binkley wrote, 'I ate most recently at TC several weeks ago, and also noticed the food seemed to have changed, and not for the better. I also got the runaround about whether he was in the kitchen . . . If in fact the photos are now gone, as reported above, I would say that it's pretty certain he is gone, too.'

But where? There were rumors about a restaurant called Hong Kong House in Richmond – or maybe that restaurant was in Virginia Beach or maybe Nashville. There were rumors that Chang might return to the suburbs of Washington, where Tim Carman, Todd Kliman's successor at the Washington *City Paper*, was complaining about how the chef's elevation to cult figure had put a damper on the local Chinese-restaurant scene. ('I have a feeling Chang will haunt Szechuan chefs in this town for a long time – or, more precisely, haunt those who have sampled Chang's cooking and will forever find other chefs wanting.') Local dining forums were searched. Restaurants were checked out. ('I called Hong Kong House in Virginia Beach,' Stephen Banker said in a post. 'No dice. Their chef hasn't changed in 12 years. The hunt goes on.') A little over a year later, in June of 2008, it was reported on the Internet that Chang had been found – at Hong Kong House, all right, but in Knoxville, Tennessee.

That was good news for Binkley: by one route, he can practically drive through Knoxville on visits to his mother, who, in her nineties, still lives in Binkley's home town of Jasper, Indiana. On the way back from those visits, he began stopping regularly at Hong Kong House. He'd have a meal, and then Chang and his wife – who handles the appetizers wherever her husband cooks – would pack up some food in a five-gallon soy-sauce bucket for him to take back to North Carolina. Binkley was told that Chang had completed one year of a five-year contract at Hong Kong House, so it appeared that the Franklin-Jasper-Knoxville-Franklin routine might last for a while. That was not to be. Last fall, between visits to his mother, Binkley was surprised to get a phone call from Mrs. Chang, who had saved a business card he'd given her. Mrs. Chang speaks better English than her husband. She was calling from Charlottesville, Virginia.

* * *

Among Changians, there has never been any shortage of theories about why their hero doesn't settle down. The most romantic one is that Peter Chang can't deal with success. Ken Flower, for one, likes that idea, although he acknowledges that it's pure conjecture. 'It seems like when the place gets built up and his reputation grows and people start coming from everywhere, he leaves,' Flower has said. People who favor that theory will point out that, as an example, Chang left Szechuan Boy only two or three weeks after Kliman's glowing review in *Washingtonian*. But, other Changians argue, isn't it more likely that what he can't deal with is not success but the flood of ignorant review-trotters that success brings – people who, radiating delight at being in the new place to be, demand a reduction of spice in a dish that's designed to be spicy or order only the sort of Americanized Chinese dishes that apparently drive Chef Chang to distraction? So could it be that the necessity of cooking inauthentic food is what drives Chef Chang away? But why would someone who dreads cooking anything but authentic Szechuan cuisine move to Knoxville?

Isn't it more likely, some Changians have argued, that he's fleeing something? What if he's in trouble with the Chinese mob – some ruthless tong that has ensnared him in who knows what sort of nefarious activity? What if he has immigration problems? During one of the periods when no one could find Chang, a post on DonRockwell.com said, 'The hunt for Peter Chang continues. It's just a question of whether we find him before la migra (immigration) does. If we do, we'll adopt him, marry him, convert him, whatever it takes.' But there is evidence that the flight scenarios are fanciful: if Chang were running, wouldn't he hide? As soon as he gets to a new restaurant, after all, he puts his prize certificates and photographs on the wall of the dining room. He cooperates with press coverage, complete with pictures. The reason for his moves, some say, must be more mundane. He may become unhappy with his working conditions – that was the case at TemptAsian, according to Kliman's Szechuan Boy review – or he may move in order to accommodate the educational needs of his daughter, who was said to be finishing high school or attending George Mason University when the Changs were in the Washington suburbs. Ken Flower's wife, Yoon-Hee Choi, counts herself a member of that practical school of thought. She speculates that Chang may be lured to each new restaurant by, say, the promise of a larger ownership share or a more favorable market potential. I was made aware of her opinion, and her husband's, while driving with them in their car on a sunny Saturday not long ago. We were on our way from Washington to Charlottesville, Virginia.

* * *

We were part of an expeditionary team gathered to try out Chang's new place of business, a restaurant on the northern edge of Charlottesville called Taste of China. Stephen Banker was also in the car; he had done the gathering. Joe Yung, whose brother is one of the proprietors of Taste of China, had arranged to drive from Fredericksburg, where he runs a more conventional Chinese restaurant, in order to act as an interpreter. John Binkley had agreed to come up from North Carolina. That would entail a drive of about seven and a half hours – not much of a journey, presumably, for an obsessed groupie Deadhead Changian like Binkley. Our trip was only about two hours, and we arrived early. Ken Flower, who had grown up in Charlottesville, took us for a quick tour of the University of Virginia's Jeffersonian grounds, and then drove back north, past a series of shopping malls that were definitely not laid out by Thomas Jefferson. In one of them, a fairly prosperous-looking collection of stores called Albemarle Square, we pulled up in front of Taste of China. It was between an H&R Block office and a place called Li'l Dino Subs. In addition to the English words, the sign had some Chinese characters. Joe Yung later told us what they meant: Szechuan Boy.

The wall we saw as we entered was properly adorned. The framed certificates were there, draped with medals. There were color photographs of Chef Chang's signature dishes – the dishes favored by customers who hadn't simply wandered in on an evening when they might just as easily have gone across the parking lot to the Outback Steakhouse. Otherwise, Taste of China looked the way a suburban restaurant of that name might be expected to look – a large room, painted a sort of salmon color, with another wall decorated with the huge glass landscape photos of China that are popular in such establishments. John Binkley's arrival (the occasion for hugs and backslaps with Chef Chang) meant that we were seven for lunch, if you count Joe Yung's American-born teenage daughter, who politely declined the spicy food she was offered and smiled graciously at remarks about how she undoubtedly preferred pizza. Yung read out a list of the dishes he'd asked the Changs to prepare, and I noticed the Changians at the table nodding along, like people at a high-school reunion listening to the best storyteller in the class relate anecdotes of the good old days. We started with some of Mrs. Chang's appetizers – Hot and Spicy Beef Rolls, which looked like burritos, and Tu Chia Style Roast Pork Meat Bread, and Scallion Bubble Pancakes, which resembled gigantic popovers, and Fish with Cilantro Rolls. There was silence at the table for a while, and then John Binkley said, 'I think she's outdone herself today. Or she's improved the craft.' I had to agree. Of course, I had never before tasted Mrs. Chang's appetizers, but, whatever they'd been like, these were definitely better.

There was equal concentration when the main courses arrived. What passes for small talk among the food-obsessed – mention of what is supposed to be an astonishing Thai restaurant in the unlikely environs of nearby Nelson County, for instance, and a short exegesis by Binkley on the origins of General Tso's Chicken – had faded as those at the table focussed on what had been set before us. Although Changians often talk about Chef Chang's use of *ma la* – the combined sensations of spiciness and numbness – the dishes were not uncomfortably hot. When I tasted the Roast Fish with Green Onions, the dish Todd Kliman had singled out in his review of Szechuan Boy, I could imagine that the Charlottesville version might have caused him to flirt with the idea of stopping by the University of Virginia to see if they'd ever considered having an eater in residence on the faculty. I was equally taken with the eggplant, which was prepared with a similar combination of spices; I could only nod (my mouth was full) when Binkley referred to Chef Chang as 'the master of cumin'. I joined in the applause when the maestro, a slight man with a big smile, came out of the kitchen. A couple of the Changians began snapping pictures, and Chang insisted on going back into the kitchen for his chef's toque before he sat down for a chat.

Some biographical details were cleared up. He's from Hubei Province, next to Szechuan Province. His father practiced traditional Chinese medicine, in which food plays a major role. His daughter, who was at Northern Virginia Community College for a while, is now studying in England. During our conversation, I got the impression that, compared with someone like Kansas City's blunt and chicken-centric Betty Lucas, Chef Chang favors complexity in discourse as well as in cooking. On the matter of why he kept moving from restaurant to restaurant, he had more answers than the Changians had theories, almost as if to say that any motivation they wanted to assign could be considered correct. Among the reasons he offered were dissatisfaction with working conditions (the kitchen at Szechuan Boy, for instance, had been too small in relation to the dining room) and the need to find effective partners and the desire to give various regions of America an opportunity to taste authentic Szechuan cooking. When Binkley, who'd spent some years in proximity to Washington politicians, heard that last one, he whispered to Ken Flower, 'That sounds like spin.'

I asked Chang if he thought that he would be in Charlottesville for a while. He hesitated, and from the Changians at the table there was what I took to be nervous laughter. Finally, he said that he liked Charlottesville, which offers a relatively sophisticated clientele, and that he thought he'd have Taste of China as a base even if he and his partners decided to open other restaurants – in Richmond, say, or even Fairfax. The mention of Fairfax brought smiles that did not seem nervous at all. I asked

Chang if he'd been aware that John Binkley and the others had launched desperate searches for him every time he disappeared. It had occurred to me that Chang might have gone from restaurant to restaurant, for ordinary or even trivial reasons, without realizing that, by some principle of physics, every small movement he made caused a huge disruption among the train of fans he was unconsciously dragging along behind him. Chef Chang smiled, and nodded. He had known about it, he said. His daughter had followed it on the Internet.

First published in the *New Yorker*, 1 March 2010

What Happened to Brie and Chablis?

What happened to Brie and Chablis?
Both Brie and Chablis used to be
The sort of thing everyone ate
When goat cheese and Napa Merlot
Weren't purchased by those in the know,
And monkfish was thought of as bait.

And why did authorities ban
From restaurants all coq au vin?
And then disappeared sole meunière,
Then banished, with little ado,
Beef Wellington – Stroganoff, too.
Then cancelled the chocolate éclair.

Then hollandaise sauce got the boot,
And kiwis stopped being the fruit
That every chef loved to include.
Like quiches, or coquilles St. Jacques,
They turned into something to mock –
The fruit that all chic chefs eschewed.

You miss, let's say, trout amandine?
Take hope from some menus I've seen:
Fondue has been spotted of late

And – yes, to my near disbelief –
Tartare not from tuna but beef.
They all may return. Just you wait.

First published in the *New Yorker*, 8 September 2003.

GREAT FOOD

A MIDDLE EASTERN FEAST
Claudia Roden

AWARD-WINNING FOOD WRITER Claudia Roden
revolutionized Western attitudes to the cuisines of the
Middle East with her bestselling *Book of Middle Eastern
Food*. Introducing millions to enticing new scents and
flavours, her intensely personal, passionate writings
conveyed an age-old tradition of family eating and shared
memory. This selection includes recipes for tagines from
Morocco, rice from Iran, peasant soup from ancient
Egypt and kofta from Armenia, as well as discussions of
spices, market bargaining, childhood memories of Cairo
and the etiquette of tea drinking; evoking not only a
cuisine but an entire way of life.

*'Roden's great gift is to conjure up not just a cuisine
but the culture from which it springs'*
NIGELLA LAWSON

··· GREAT FOOD ···

RECIPES AND LESSONS FROM A DELICIOUS COOKING REVOLUTION

Alice Waters

A CHAMPION OF ORGANIC, locally produced and seasonal food and founder of acclaimed Californian restaurant Chez Panisse, Alice Waters has recently been awarded the *Légion d'honneur* in France for her contributions to food culture. In this book, she explores the simplest of dishes in the most delicious of ways, with fresh, sustainable ingredients a must, even encouraging cooks to plant their own garden.

From orange and olive salad to lemon curd and ginger snaps, Waters constantly emphasizes the joys and ease of cooking with local, fresh food, whether in soups, salads or sensual, classic desserts.

'Waters is a legend'
JAY RAYNER

····· GREAT FOOD ·····

A TASTE OF THE SUN

Elizabeth David

LEGENDARY COOK AND WRITER Elizabeth David changed the way Britain ate, introducing a postwar nation to the sun-drenched delights of the Mediterranean, and bringing new flavours and aromas such as garlic, wine and olive oil into its kitchens.

This mouthwatering selection of her writings and recipes embraces the richness of French and Italian cuisine, from earthy cassoulets to the simplest spaghetti, as well as evoking the smell of buttered toast, the colours of foreign markets and the pleasures of picnics. Rich with anecdote, David's writing is defined by a passion for good, authentic, well-balanced food that still inspires chefs today.

'Above all, Elizabeth David's books make you want to cook'
TERENCE CONRAN

GREAT FOOD

LOVE IN A DISH
& OTHER PIECES
M. F. K. Fisher

M. F. K. FISHER'S PERSONAL, intimate culinary
essays are well-loved American classics, combining
recipes with her anecdotes, reminiscences, cultural
observations and passionate storytelling.

Hailed as 'poet of the appetites' by John Updike
and considered the greatest American prose writer by
W. H. Auden, Fisher saw eating as inextricably bound
up with living well. Whether reflecting on an epic lunch
served by a fanatical waitress, the life-giving properties
of wine, quails whose glorious smell 'would rouse Lazarus'
or how the love of food can save a marriage, each
piece is a perfectly crafted work of art.

'Poet of the appetites'
JOHN UPDIKE

···· GREAT **FOOD** ····

BUFFALO CAKE AND INDIAN PUDDING

Dr A. W. Chase

TRAVELLING PHYSICIAN, SALESMAN, author and self-made man, Dr Chase dispensed remedies all over America during the late nineteenth century, collecting recipes and domestic tips from the people he met along the way. His self-published books became celebrated US bestsellers and were the household bibles of their day.

Containing recipes for American-style treats, such as Boston cream cakes, Kentucky corn dodgers and pumpkin pie, as well as genial advice on baking bread and testing whether a cake is cooked, this is a treasure trove of culinary wisdom from the homesteads of a still rural, pioneering United States.

GREAT  FOOD

THROUGHOUT the history of civilization, food has been livelihood, status symbol, entertainment – and passion. The twenty fine food writers here, reflecting on different cuisines from across the centuries and around the globe, have influenced each other and continue to influence us today, opening the door to the wonders of every kitchen.